Illumination by Darkness

The Reshaping of Psychoanalysis
From Sigmund Freud to Ernest Becker

Barry R. Arnold
General Editor

Vol. 1

PETER LANG
New York • San Francisco • Bern
Frankfurt am Main • Berlin • Wien • Paris

Bernard J. Bergen

Illumination by Darkness

Freud and the Social Bond

PETER LANG
New York • San Francisco • Bern
Frankfurt am Main • Berlin • Wien • Paris

Library of Congress Cataloging-in-Publication Data

Bergen, Bernard J.
    Illumination by darkness : Freud and the social bond / by Bernard J. Bergen.
        p. cm. — (The Reshaping of psychoanalysis ; v. 1)
    Includes bibliographical references.
    1. Psychoanalysis—History. 2. Social psychology—History. 3. Freud, Sigmund, 1856-1939. I. Title. II. Series.
BF173.B467 1992   150.19'52—dc20   91-33002
ISBN 0-8204-1759-9   CIP
ISSN 1059-3551

Die Deutsche Bibliothek-CIP-Einheitsaufnahme

Bergen, Bernard J.:
Illumination by darkness : Freud and the social bond / Bernard J. Bergen.—New York; Berlin; Bern; Frankfurt/M.; Paris; Wien: Lang, 1992
    (The reshaping of psychoanalysis ; Vol. 1)
    ISBN 0-8204-1759-9
NE: GT

Permissions credits are located on pages 150 an 151 of this book.

Cover Design by Jim Brisson.

The paper in this book meets the guidelines for permanence and durability of the Committee on Production Guidelines for Book Longevity of the Council on Library Resources.

© Peter Lang Publishing, Inc., New York 1992

All rights reserved.
Reprint or reproduction, even partially, in all forms such as microfilm, xerography, microfiche, microcard, offset strictly prohibited.

Printed in the United States of America.

Table of Contents

Acknowledgements vii

Introduction ix

Part One: Famous Last Words 1

Part Two: Reversals 31

Part Three: Sartre's Passion 67

Part Four: Freud's Last Word 115

Acknowledgements

I have the great fortune of having friends who keep showing me the inestimable value of discourse while teaching me what discourse really is: Lou and Crista Renza, Claude Thomas, and Bill Arney.

I am also grateful to Don Pease whose critique of the manuscript meant more to me than he suspects; to Dan Krymkowski who gave me his personal support during hard times, and to Stan Rosenberg who helped me understand much about psychoanalysis.

I also owe a great deal to Michael Flamini's editorial confidence in the manuscript which brought the project to its fruition.

This book is dedicated to Vera, who keeps teaching me, as she has throughout what amounts to my lifetime, with patience and love, that there is a world out there that must be lived.

sometimes the otter and sometimes the hound
                                              Peter Weiss, Marat/Sade

I was capable, I knew it before he did, although he gave me more than confirmation when he said it, he made me his.
                                          E. L. Doctorow, "Billy Bathgate".

The vital question remains - what or who is King Kong?
                    Grahame Green, "The Captain and the Enemy".

Introduction

Our century requires us to understand what Freud tells us about ourselves in his own terms, rather than filtered through the screen of the history of psychoanalytic thought which is a revisionist history.

With respect to this history, there is a diverse group of revisionists who represent themselves as part of a general project to complete psychoanalytic theory. This includes such prominent psychoanalytic names as Anna Freud and Melanie Klein, as well as such banished "deviationists" as Adler, Jung, and Reich, who carried elements of Freud's work into new psychoanalytic forms, and Binswanger, Sartre, and Lacan for whom completing Freud becomes a matter of thinking through, from different but not entirely uncoordinated directions, everything in his work from the ground up. This diverse group tends to see their project as the same one Freud himself began with meetings of the first psychoanalytic society held in his Vienna apartment. Lacan's call for a return to Freud in the sense of a "return to the spirit of the text..."[1], treated purely as a slogan that brackets both its polemical thrust and the specific theoretical content to which it alludes, can serve as the emblem for the history of psychoanalytic theorizing that evolved from that beginning. The continuing history of completing Freud's work was, from the first, a revisionist project that would ultimately leave virtually no concept or idea untouched while proceeding from the starting point Freud chose to carry the psychoanalytic imprimatur.

Freud's starting point, of course, was a call to patients to make the confused experience of their suffering coherent by a work of consciousness that would displace the meaning of the world they were conscious of into a region of unconscious meanings. If Freud was not the first to attempt to make suffering coherent in terms of a theory about how unconscious desires which, pursued by subjects, alienate them from their possibilities in the world, he certainly marked an entire age of Western culture with his name. Freud calling his patients to a work of consciousness was the starting point for restructuring a discourse on suffering which had already exhausted itself in a "tradition extending from Plato to Kant through Christian Platonism..." - a tradition which "fails to locate suffering with respect to the purposive activity of a human subject, identifying it instead with distance or alienation from an ideal order." [2]

But what is there about Freud's work that prompts its completion by revision? Almost all revisionist readings assume at bottom that Freud's starting point makes his work something like a promissory note that fails to deliver the liberation of subjects from a confusion about the meaning of their suffering that strangles their possibilities. In this sense, the history of psychoanalytic theorizing can be thought of as a history of revising Freud's work to complete its promise by making it adequate to its starting point. They assume as well, much the same kind of story behind his failure. Breger has recently captioned that story with the title of his book: "Freud's Unfinished Journey". Describing Freud's work as the product of a 19th Century culture whose values and education it could not reasonably be expected to surpass, Breger observes that "while Freud is a transitional figure... the transition is never fully realized in his own work. There is a continual mixing of old and new assumptions, of progress to a fresh viewpoint and regression to the old, of radically new modes of understanding stated in a cumbersome language of the past. Hence, the unfinished journey." [3]

The plaint which underwrites the revisionist history of reading Freud is that the journey his work fails to complete is toward a vision of possibility which must guide its call to a work of consciousness. Even the narrowest clinical reading of Freud's work which limits its value to grounding the technique of therapy with patients finds itself struggling to formulate such a vision. Janet Malcolm's interviews with her now famous respondent, "Adam Green", for instance, for whom psychoanalytic theory seems to come alive only during the psychoanalytic hour, often comes down to a debate over the nature of human possibility.[4] It is a debate with strong echoes from the past. On one level, the history of completing psychoanalytic theory is a history of the same debate conducted at different times with different players.

Freud's work, in fact, never does present us with a vision of human possibility that defines a subject's recovery from the confused experience of suffering. This makes his work appear as if its originality is dispersed by a beginning that does not lead to the end it must contain. In other words it appears to be a fragmented theory that fails to fulfill the conditions for narrative coherency - something like a story whose events are difficult to follow and make sense of because they cannot be followed to an end.

Revisionists assume that only a vision of human possibility can make psychoanalysis a coherent fulfillment of Freud's original promise of liberation, but they do not assume that psychoanalysis must bear the burden alone. Indeed, they assume the opposite because a vision of possibility that completes psychoanalysis must be a vision defined by the structure of the social world as a kind of theatre of possibility to which subjects' developmental history binds them, or, in the case of patients, fails to bind them. The revisionist history of psychoanalytic theorizing is a history of completing Freud by locating psychoanalysis as a specialized discipline grounded in a specialized theory about the essential development of individuals' bonding to society. The Behavioral Sciences have long acknowleged that whatever terms, and by whatever interdisciplinary collaboration a vision of human possibility is formulated, it must be tightly interwoven with psychoanalytic theory. By the same token, it is generally recognized by most psychoanalytic revisionists that psychoanalytic theory is tightly interwoven with socio-political questions of how to make the social world conform to a vision of human possibility which must guide its call to a work of consciousness.

The referent for that 19th century beginning which fails both Freud and psychoanalysis is familiar. It is the often explicit and always implicit focus for the revision of his work: the instinctual doctrine which grounds his theorizing. One of Freud's most persistent tropes for describing his own theorizing is the metaphor of an archaeological work. It appears in his last paper, "Constructions in Analysis", and in his first great work, "The Interpretation of Dreams", where he notes at the end of his theoretical Chapter 7, "we have been obliged to build our way out into the dark. If we are not wholly in error, other lines of approach are bound to lead us into much the same region and the time may then come when we shall find ourselves more at home in it."[5] The use of this archaelogical metaphor can be read as the cautionary call of the scientist reminding us of the hesitant openness that a scientific theory of psychoanalysis must maintain before declaring a closure on Truth. But it can also be read in another way which is more consonant with the direction in which Freud's own theory moves. The displacement of conscious meaning is always the starting point for uncovering the secret history of a subject's desires by interpreting a chain of substitute meanings that trace the history of the purposes the desiring subject pursues back to their origin in the vicissitudes of the instincts.

The vicissitudes of the instincts is a history which is always played out in the dark because Freud's concept of "instincts" does not refer to hypothetical constructs designed to account for biological events in a subject's history of desiring. Instincts substitute for the subject as the intentional agent who produces meaning, and to which intention's meaning must be reduced if it is to be made coherent. Jacob Needleman sums it up concisely: "It is essential to note that this basic reality of psychoanalysis, the drives or instincts, although a concept arising strictly from the science of biology, is a purposive intentional reality. An instinct intends an object; it is not, like the objective processes, say, of physics something in itself possessing no meaning or reference beyond itself and needing the theorizing of the physics to relate it conclusively with other data. An instinct points beyond itself to its satisfaction...Thus in Freud, phenomena of consciousness, themselves intentional, are reduced to instincts, also intentional...The essential reference of intentionality to an agent-self is erased by postulating in its stead a form of intentionality (instinctuality) for which the reference to an agent-self is not constitutive." [6]

Freud's work is a constant, and sometimes tortuously convoluted thinking through of the history of subjects' desires as a history of the vicissitudes of the instincts. Freud describes this history by deploying the intentionality of the instincts in dramatic stories about the origins of desire that take place in the region of darkness into which we are called to "build out". We are building out into the dark regions where myths live in the hope that we will find ourselves at home there so that we can interpretively read the scenes of this world. Freud's story about the "primal horde" is not the product of a creative mind which could not resist wandering into imaginative speculations about the origins of things. It is not an isolated side story in Freud's work about the origins of religion as a social institution, but a story about the origin of the social bond, for which religion must serve as the paradigm. The primal horde story is intended to illuminate no less than how "events took the course we so often see them follow in human affairs to this day."[7] It is a story which does not begin with an oppressive father denying the possibilities of freedom for his sons, but with the sons' ambivalence toward their father which must play itself out in his murder and the subsequent remorseful "wish to identify themselves with him" which restores the "dead father... stronger than the living one had been..." as the foundation for the social bond.[8] It is intended to illuminate history as a repetitive movement fueled by a fragile covenant with Hope in the form of a Law of Possibility which must always conceal the face of the Father as the object of destructive envy. But it is also a story which points to another story about the origins of the social bond in terms of the vicissitudes of the instincts. The ambivalence that precedes desire and governs the changing scenes of history is an ambivalence troped in "Beyond the Pleasure Principle" as a "little fragment of living substance ... suspended in the middle of an external world charged with the most powerful energies..."[9] that is forced into enduring life. It is the conflict between Eros and the death instinct that governs the history of the world.

Freud, using the language of myth - "imagery and personification"[10] - to present the vicissitudes of the instincts, presents more than simply stories about the origin of events. The narrative forms of myths, to use Kenneth Burke's terms, are ways of "propounding principles of governance by translation".[11] For Freud, this is invariably a question of translating confused experience into what is tellable. Freud's myths function as frames for ordering confused experience at the level of meaning.

But while Freud's myths are like allegories, they are not simply allegorical renditions of the human condition. They are not meant to be narratives subject to the ambiguities of meaning that invite further interpretation. The search for a myth that expresses a governing principle for the translation of experience does not lead, as it does with Burke, to a grammar of motives and a grammar of rhetoric. Freud demands that if experience is to be made coherent, it must be referred to governing principles that are outside language. Freud's myths about the vicissitudes of the instincts supply this finality of reference for rendering experience meaningful. Borch-Jacobsen puts his finger directly on this in his study critical of the idea in Freud's work of an instinctual agency. At the end of his study, Borch-Jacobsen, citing the strategic importance of the primal horde story in "Group Psychology and the Analysis of the Ego", observes: "We are left, then, with a myth. For it would be pointless to try to comment on this at once intimidating and derisory myth. In a way, there is nothing to seek beyond what it says. It says what it says, no more and no less. It states, dictates, decrees, institutes the Political (and the) Subject."[12]

The vicissitudes of the instincts can be known only by being represented in myths that illuminate history from the dark as repetition compulsion; history reduced to the repetition of the primal horde story as the return of the repressed - always a new son stepping forward to complete the revolt which, as the myth tells, is destined to endlessly fail. The primal horde story is repeated in every social bond; and every social bond is a passion which assigns to another the identity of the world. The return of the repressed is what haunts the social bond, as Freud tells us in his last great published work, "Moses and Monotheism", which is clearly myth thinly disguised as history. The return of the repressed demands coordinating the primal horde myth with the myth of Eros and the death instinct, the drama in which instinctual energies play out the drama of the social bond apparent to Freud in every patient's transference: desire's conflict over needing but not wanting the world. It is as if the scenes of history appear on an illuminated stage governed by a drama that goes on in the dark somewhere offstage.

Reading Freud means finding oneself increasingly caught up in the same story about another world which this one represents. The dramas enacted by the primal horde and Eros and the death instinct are the foundation of "The Ego and the Id", and Freud's sociological texts, "Civilization and its Discontents", and "Group Psychology and the Analysis of the Ego" cannot be understood except through "The Ego and the Id". Freud never stops exploring the scenes being played out in those dark regions where myth is at home. His work takes as its starting point the call to subjects to do a work of consciousness which uncovers the true meaning of their suffering, and then presents this truth in the form of an aporia. "This is where the aporia arises" Ricoeur points out, "what is the status of representation or ideas in relation to the notions of instinct, aim of instinct and affect? How can an interpretation of meaning through meaning be integrated with an economics of cathexis, withdrawal of cathexis, anticathexis? At first glance, there seems to be an antinomy between an explanation governed by the principles of the metapsychology and an interpretation that necessarily moves among meanings and not among forces, among representations or ideas, and not among instincts." [13]

With the notable exception of Ricoeur's own reading of Freud, that "first glance" is what animates the history of revising Freud's work. Freud not only never tries to resolve the aporia, but increasingly accentuates it, with bolder and bolder mythological tales about the origins of desire as the vicissitudes of the instincts leaving his work increasingly vulnerable to the charge of confused incoherency.

But the record shows that Freud was well aware of this vulnerability. To cite an instance, he wrote to Lou Andreas-Salome, who frequently importuned him to integrate his ideas, "I so rarely feel the need for synthesis." [14] It was a strange thing for Freud to have said, since he had already written "Beyond the Pleasure Principle", which is a synthesizing theoretical work about which he was to state to Ernest Jones, that no matter how much it was criticized, he could no longer see without it. [15] "Beyond the Pleasure Principle" reviews everything psychoanalysis had discovered to that point to discover a remainder to what it knew which it proceeds to integrate into a psychoanalytic theory that could then claim to know the origin and course of human life. Freud was building the architectonic of his work toward an ending which he could already see, and whose outline he may well have seen at its beginning.

Can there be a connection between Freud's resistance to revisionist demands that, to one extent or another, he sacrifice the elaboration of the mythological narratives through which he represents his instinctual doctrine, and a movement of his work toward an ending which would give it coherency on its own terms as a call to a work of consciousness? In other words, does Freud's work move toward a cohering end by resisting revisionist demands that the subject of psychoanalytic theory be the human subject and not the vicissitudes of the instincts?

This book takes up the question of this connection. Admittedly, this involves a reading of Freud's work which must bear the burden of its peculiarities. First, Freud's work cannot escape justifying itself as a call to a subject to perform a work of consciousness. The conscious subject cannot be made to disappear as both the starting and end point of psychoanalytic theory without making psychoanalytic theory disappear. Yet Freud's theory can only move from its starting point to an ending in which subjects clarify the meaning of their confused suffering in terms of the mythic structures that represent their history as the history of the vicissitudes of the instincts. Second, it involves tracing the movement in Freud's work toward this peculiar ending through a series of negations of its revisionist readings that move it toward a visionary end which they define as constitutive of a coherent psychoanalytic theory.

But perhaps this does not make for such a peculiar reading, after all. Harold Bloom argues that "the precursors of Freud are not so much Charcot and Janet, Brucke and Helmholtz, Breuer and Fliess, but rather more exalted company of Empedocles and Heraclitus, Plato and Goethe, Shakespeare and Schopenhauer".[16] Stated as a way of reading Freud, this view is surely open to argument. But Bloom also means to state something about Freud's ambition which seems true enough. Freud belongs to that group Bloom calls "strong poets, major figures with the persistence to wrestle with their strong precursors, even to the death. Weaker talents idealize; figures of capable imagination appropriate for themselves. But nothing is got for nothing, and self appropriation involves the immense anxieties of indebtedness, for what strong maker desires the realization that he has failed to create himself?"[17] This is a worthy description of Freud's ambition. He surely intended a theory that would be no less than, in Bloom's terms, the "beginning of a canonical tradition." Alongside "the Yahwist, the strongest writer in the Bible, and Homer... we can place Freud, whose agon with the whole of anteriority is the largest and most intense of our century." [18]

The impossibility that such an ambition to be radically original can be "got for nothing", goes some distance toward accounting for Freud's conflict over speaking plainly about the ending toward which he aimed his work. The stakes of his struggle are high: To end his work by defining the justification for his own invention, psychoanalysis, outside the frame of the clinical promise that founded it - that subjects alienated from their agency would recover it through a work of consciousness. Freud sends many signals that he was conflicted over exploring and elaborating mythological narratives as the only terms in which his work could be given a coherent ending. It is more than a matter of personal style that he embroiders them with hesitations, uncertainties and doubts.

This book, however, is not an attempt to explore Freud's psychology, but to trace the movement of his work toward its ending by examining the series of negating excesses it presents that oppose what can be called the normalizing ground on which the revisionist history of psychoanalytic theorizing transposes his work to complete it.

A brief introductory sketch of this movement is in order, as well as a sketch of the end toward which it aims and what is put at stake as the very definition of psychoanalysis as a call to a work of consciousness.

Freud's resistance to substituting for the mythic dramas about the vicissitudes of the instincts played out in the darkness that is like another world which this one represents, a vision of human possibility identified with the making and remaking of the social history of this world, does not mean that his work fails to lead to an ending which presents conscious subjects retrieving the truth of their suffering. It is an ending, however, which presents a conscious subject who remains where he was when he began the work of retrieving the truth of his suffering - experiencing a confusion over suffering a separation from his agency. Nowhere in Freud's work, grounded throughout in his instinctual doctrine, is suffering transcended. The confused experience of suffering is retrieved only as confusion seen clearly as confusion, and not as confusion clarified.

To follow Freud's work to this end is to follow the passion of the transference moved out of the clinic into the world as the world. The social bond is not like the scene of the transference; it is that scene arising out of a play of forces over which subjects have no agential control. Freud always talks about the human world as a social bond forged by love, yet he never talks about love outside the frame of the transference. In Freud, there is no "outside" to that frame; the frame is identical to the human world repeated as the scene of the transference. Freud never denies that the history of the world is a history of different scenes unfolding in time, anymore than he denies that the scene of the transference in therapy has a history. But the differences are differences that make no difference. The meaning of the scenes of history change, but the meaning of the changes always refers us to a repetition of the single scene of the transference which accounts for the world.

The end toward which Freud's work moves which guides the work of consciousness he invented under the name of psychoanalysis, is a scandalous warning about love. Freud's work calls us to move the transference into the world as the world, and this calls us to interpret all our loves, including our love of the most abstract vision of human possibility which can be offered as a guide to subjects' recovering their agency, as representations of the forces that drive us to impossible passions. Freud calls us to demystify our most treasured myths of love as a healing force privileged from suspicion which bonds us to the world as our possibility. Love must be placed under the sign of suspicion because it is passion concealed as love which puts the world into jeopardy. Freud, the agonist, wrestles his revisionists' canonical reading of his work to make the problem of the social bond his own by defining the jeopardy of the world in terms of subjects living the illusion of themselves as the agents who must make the world conform to a vision of possibility they love with a love privileged from suspicion.

Freud is not a great transitional figure between the 19th and 20th centuries; his work carries him into the agenda of the 20th century. It is Hannah Arendt's attempts to understand the Nazi movement and the "Final Solution" that can be said to represent that agenda. In her "Origins of Totalitarianism" Arendt declares, in effect, that understanding the Nazi movement means understanding that its death camps were not simply its by-products, but the definition of its purpose. They were the "laboratories for verifying its most fundamental beliefs". Everything else was of "secondary importance".[19] The ultimate horror testified to by Holocaust witnesses is that the production of corpses was tenaciously continued at the very end when it could no longer make any sense at all. Sense had to be resisted and the senseless pursued, something all psychoanalysts face with their patients; phenomena which Freud identified as "resistance" and pondered not as a failure of technique, but as a phenomenon that originates with the vicissitudes of the instincts that commands our agency.

Arendt sees that the starting point for understanding the origins of totalitarianism which puts the world into jeopardy cannot simply be a confused people pursuing false visions of the possibilities offered by the social bond. The starting point must be a human world whose defining characteristic is to always be in jeopardy because it arises from and depends on the social bond. This is the full significance of her search for a *cura posterior* by coming face to face with Eichmann in Jerusalem,[20] where she dared to see in that encounter, the Final Solution within the framework of the "banality of evil."[21] It is a daring framework which demands that we see Eichmann and the Jews - victimizer and victims - mirroring each other as reflections of the terrible threats inherent in the social bond, and that through her own search for a *cura posterior*, we see ourselves in that reflection.

Arendt, of course, is a political and not a psychoanalytic thinker. But to whom shall we turn but to Freud to understand the warning she sounds about the social bond - a warning she clearly sees in our time must wear the face of Eichmann? It is time to see Freud's myths not as side stories, but as an attempt to illuminate the world from a darkness that allows us to think through from the beginning the subject of the jeopardy of the world. Freud, by seeking to make the problem of the social bond his own, produced a body of work by thinking against his revisionists from the very beginning, and Freud's revisionists, from the very beginning have always accused his work of lacking an answer to the question "Where is Hope?" But Freud's work leads to his sociological texts which assert that the question is the wrong one. Hope is everywhere because the structure of the world arises everywhere from the passion of the social bond, and passion is like a force over which we have no agential control. We are, to use one of Freud's earliest but always trenchant metaphors of the mind, like a machine which runs by itself, producing Hope. At the same time it is possible to see the confusion of passion for what it is: As our century knows only too well passion, when it deceives itself with the name of love privileged from suspicion, can be like a machine which produces corpses that fill the world.

And yet, the end toward which Freud's work moves, the warning about love, cannot quite be the end. It is an end in which there still remains the tension between Freud the theoretician and Freud the clinician. The transference is unalterable because fantasy is unalterable. Passion is unalterable because that is what we are as fantasy. Yet there is something further that can be said about that work of consciousness which puts love under the sign of suspicion and which is the only edge we have against ourselves to preserve the world. Kristeva suggests it:

> "Analysis strictly speaking exacts payment of the price set by the subject for revealing that his or her complaints, symptoms or fantasies are discourses of love directed to an impossible other - always unsatisfactory, transitory, incapable of meeting my wants or desires. Yet by revealing to my analyst the wants and desires I feel, I give them access to the powers of speech and at the same time bring the powers of speech into ostensibly nameless recesses of meaning. Thus I gain access to my symptoms; I orchestrate my fantasies or I eliminate them, sometimes ably, sometimes less so."[22]

Only a work of consciousness which, by putting love under the sign of suspicion, can turn fantasy against itself. What else is maturity but endlessly dissolving a fantastic self posited to deliver gestures of loyalty to the Father in the form of corpses, in the hope he will return our love, breathing life into us as if for the first time? Endlessly, because what else did Freud try to teach us but that we stop dissolving that fantastic self with the mysteriously unfathomable power of consciousness at the risk of loving a final solution to the pain of living by believing that there is a Father who will actually love us in the way we fantasize our passion for that love?

*****

This book is divided into four parts:

Part 1, "Famous Last Words", interprets the abounding judgements that Freud's work is fragmented, without a syncretic center and lacking a coherent narrative structure. These judgements are interpreted as expressons of frustration over Freud's resistance to fulfilling the liberating promise of psychoanalysis by supplying a vision of human possibility as an end to his work. This opposition between Freud and the revisionist project to complete him that defines the history of psychoanalytic theorizing from its beginning is presented through an analysis of one of his last great texts, "Analysis Terminable and Interminable" which sounds the theme constant over his entire work: The movement of the transference out of the clinic into the world is the social bond which makes the human world possible.

Part 2, "Reversals", starts with a reading of Freud's cases, "Dora", "The Rat Man", and "The Wolf Man", from the point of view of their importance for defining the transference as the paradigm of the social bond. These cases are analyzed to show how the location of two of the critical conceptual elements of psychoanalytic theory out of which the social bond is forged, anxiety and ambivalence, are located by Freud in a narrative about human development that opposes revisionist narratives. Freud's developmental narrative is coordinated with the "primal horde myth" in "Totem and Taboo", which points to his most obscure text, "Beyond the Pleasure Principle" in which he articulates the vicissitudes of the instincts in terms of the conflict between Eros and the death instinct, as the origin of the social bond. A close reading of "Beyond the Pleasure Principle" is presented to show that it is a coherent rather than aberrant text when it is read as a cautionary tale about passion which moves his theory toward a cautionary last word that is a warning about love at the foundation of the social bond.

Part 3, "Sartre's Passion", puts into relief the critical role which privileging love from suspicion plays in the revisionist paradigm by a reading of Sartre as a psychoanalytic revisionist. The movement of Sartre's work from a beginning that is as insistent and powerful a call to consciousness as Freud's to place love under the sign of suspicion, to a paean to love at the end which echoes the revisionist paradigm of completing Freud, is traced through Sartre's "biographies" of Baudelaire, Genet, and Flaubert. These "biographies", almost never treated seriously in critical readings of Sartre, become coherent when they are read as following the principles that govern the construction of psychoanalytic case histories, and reveal the narrative strategies of the revisionist paradigm for completing Freud with a vision of possibility that fulfills the promise of a social bond based on love.

Part 4, "Freud's Last Word", interprets three of Freud's late texts, "The Ego and the Id", "Civilization and Its Discontents", and "Group Psychology and the Analysis of the Ego", as culminating the movement of his work toward its last unifying word of a warning about love at the foundation of the social bond. The significance of this warning is interpreted in terms of how it reconfigures the justification of psychoanalysis as a work of consciousness that can discover the truth of Hope, to a work of consciousness that calls subjects to valorize the confusion they must live if they are to preserve the world. The significance of this call that ends Freud's work, lies in placing him at the center of the agenda of the twentieth century represented by Hannah Arendt's attempt to understand the social bond as the banality of evil by confronting Eichmann in Jerusalem.

References

1. Anthony Wilden, *The Language of the Self*, Baltimore, The Johns Hopkins Press, 1968, p. ix.

2. Mary C. Rawlinson, "The Sense of Suffering", *The Journal of Medicine and Philosophy*, 11:1 1986, p. 40.

3. Louis Breger, *Freud's Unfinished Journey*, London, Routledge & Kegan Paul, 1981, p. 4.

4. Janet Malcolm, *Psychoanalysis: The Impossible Profession*, New York, Vintage Books, 1982.

5. Sigmund Freud, *The Interpretation of Dreams*, tr. James Strachey, New York, Basic Books, 1955, p. 511.

6. Jacob Needleman, "A Critical Introduction to Ludwig Binswanger's Existential Psychoanalysis", in *Being in the World: Selected Papers of Ludwig Binswanger*, tr. Jacob Needleman, New York, Harper Torchbooks, 1967, p. 51-52.

7. Sigmund Freud, "Totem and Taboo", *Standard Edition*, V. 13, p. 143.

8. Ibid., p. 143.

9. Sigmund Freud, "Beyond the Pleasure Principle", *Standard Edition*, V. 18, p. 27.

10. Kenneth Burke, *Language as Symbolic Action*, Berkeley, University of California Press, 1966, p. 391.

11. Ibid., p. 381.

12. Mikkel Borch-Jacobsen, *The Freudian Subject*, tr. Catherine Porter, Stanford California, Stanford University Press, 1988, p. 237.

13. Paul Ricoeur, *Freud and Philosophy*, tr. Denis Savage, New Haven, Yale University Press, 1970, p. 66.

14. Ernst Pfeiffer, ed., *Sigmund Freud and Lou Andreas-Salome: Letters*, tr. William and Elaine Robson-Scott, London, Hogarth, 1972, p. 32.

15. Ernest Jones, *The Life and Work of Sigmund Freud*, edited and abridged by Lionel Trilling and Steven Marcus, New York, Basic Books, 1961, p. 407.

16. Harold Bloom, *Agon: Towards a Theory of Revisionism*, New York, Oxford University Press, 1982, p. 91.

17. Harold Bloom, *The Anxiety of Influence*, New York, Oxford University Press, 1973, p. 5.

18. Harold Bloom, *The Breaking of the Vessels*, Chicago, The University of Chicago Press, 1982, p. 47.

19. Hannah Arendt, *The Origins of Totalitarianism*, New York, Harvest/HBJ Books, 1973, p. 437-438.

20. Elisabeth Young-Bruehl, *Hannah Arendt: For Love of the World*, New Haven, Yale University Press, 1982, p. 331.

21. Hannah Arendt, *Eichmann in Jerusalem: A Report on the Banality of Evil*, New York, The Viking Press, 1963.

22. Julia Kristeva, *In the Beginning was Love: Psychoanalysis and Faith*, tr. Arthur Goldhammer, New York, Columbia University Press, 1987, p. 7.

Part One

Famous Last Words

In 1902 Freud summoned Adler, Stekel, Kahane and Reitler, four somewhat eccentric Jewish physicians in an eccentric fin-de-siecle Vienna, to help him begin a history of psychoanalysis. Freud did not parse out specific problems for his disciples to solve, although this was how the scientific laboratories of his time organized research. They were summoned less as acolytes to deliver the word than as colleagues who would help formulate it. Freud wore the badge of power, the privilege of having the last word, at those first Wednesday meetings. The beginning belonged to him alone, and therefore he had the right to protect it, oversee its development and above all, will the terms of its destiny. Freud's last word was almost invariably a cautionary word. He mainly praised hesitation and extolled the personal virtues of diffidence. He counseled that the meaning of his ideas are convoluted, their referents complicated, and their implications not always what they appear to be.

Freud's power over the last word was a power to frustrate. Stekel, for example, tells us that at those first discussions in Freud's apartment, "a spark seemed to jump from one mind to the other, and every evening was like a revelation. We were so enthralled..."[1] Freud's ideas struck fire in the minds of men which could not be contained by cautionary last words that diffused their meaning. Stekel is seized by a spark and carves out the study of the symbol as his province. It is the word which holds an original power over the world. Stekel will give psychoanalytic theory the organizing focus which Freud seemed unsure about. Only psychoanalysis can solve the mystery of why the word is never spoken plainly. Psychoanalytic theory will mediate the transfer of the power of the word to the world. The crooked will be made straight.

Freud does not encourage Stekel's work. At one Wednesday meeting, for example, Freud criticizes him for relying "exclusively on his inspirations, instead of submitting them to the control of conscious thinking".[2] The "exclusively" is an exaggeration of how Stekel is going about synthesizing Freud's fragmented ideas. Freud's remonstration is surely something like a cruel irony, from someone who had already attested to drawing inspiration from his own unconscious to solve the mystery of the dream, and was committed to more than a passing interest in the occult.

We must see more in Freud's cautionary stance toward synthesizing his work than solely a strategy for preventing eager, ambitious and sometimes erratic disciples from turning psychoanalysis into an intellectual scandal. Freud's own uncertainties and hesitations at the beginning suffuse the entire corpus of his written work, giving it the appearance of confused incompleteness. It is a frustrating work to read Freud. Mahony, looking at his work through contemporary eyes, sees in it a "deep rooted fragmentation. . .in. . .thought and procedure."[3] Today Freud's texts seem to function analogously to his last cautionary words at those first Wednesday discussions. Mahony, describing the "processive composition" of Freud's "Wolf Man" case as something like "a do-it-yourself kit", goes on to remark that "its ongoingness is part and parcel of Freud's fundamental conception of psychoanalysis as an incomplete discipline to which he significantly contributed by fragmentary essays, by fragmentary case histories and theorizations, but never once by a comprehensive psychology".[4] He concludes that a "linear reading of Freud is too simplistic . . ." We must read him by combining "multiple perspectives" because his work reads like "clinical material, with nodal points, associations, retrospective glances at past remarks, and anticipations of what is to follow".[5]

Laplanche and Pontalis share this judgment. Their impressive dictionary of Freud's concepts comes down in the end to "fighting ... with words" in order to find "behind the words ... facts, ideas, and the conceptual organization of psychoanalysis".[6] They confess that it is "only by offering an *interpretation* can we hope to trace certain constant structures of psychoanalytical thought and experience as they pass though transformations...Our commentary has striven to dispel or at any rate make plain the ambiguities of the principal notions, to expose their contradictory aspects".[7] In effect, Laplanche and Pontalis, by inserting their own commentary into the spaces between Freud's concepts, and between different meanings of the same concepts, expose the question that the history of psychoanalytic thought has always chewed on to nourish itself: "What is it that Freud is really getting at?" In a similar vein Roustang tropes Freud's work as having a "nervous center".[8] Discontinuity seems to be the rule: "If you attempt to consider the body of Freud's work as a whole, as you could do for Spinoza, Kant or Hegel, you will understand nothing at all. This is even true for each idea taken separately." All you will find are "variations in meaning and often contradictions that cannot be resolved or synthesized".[9]

Freud never cooperated to relieve others' frustrations over reading his work. Lou Andreas-Salome, for instance, who loved Freud as he did her, never fails to tell him how far ahead of her he is in his thinking, although she is always ahead of him, anticipating a synthesizing last word. Freud points this out to her in one of his letters: "Every time I read one of your letters of appraisal I am amazed at your talent for going beyond what has been said, the completing it and making it converge at some distant point. Naturally I do not always agree with you. I so rarely feel the need for synthesis".[10]

Lou does feel that need because for her, Freud's work is incomplete without a holistic view of the conflicting forces that are the constant reference points for his theorizing. Her frustration is over his unwillingness to take the last step to revise his thinking in dialectical terms. In a letter to Freud, after reading "Beyond the Pleasure Principle", a text which is often thought of as his most arcane, she presents her revision of its thesis concerning the conflict between the life and death instincts: "Death and life stand in a mutual relationship to one another, of which the whole is inevitably concealed from us. Each is half of one and the same event; just as the invisible half of the moon forms a mysterious integral part of our total lunar concept."[11] She is retracing a gentle chiding she had given Freud two years earlier: "And when you say, as you are fond of saying, that you are satisfied with the fragmentary, at a deeper level it is clear how little it is really a question of the fragmentary, and how the unifying factor emerges unsought and of itself precisely from your method of procedure".[12] It is, interestingly enough, the same charge repeated in a more dense and sophisticated way more than a quarter century later by Norman O. Brown in "Life Against Death".[13] Freud never directly responded to Lou's reading of "Beyond the Pleasure Principle." Had he done so, it probably would not have been too different from the response he had written four years earlier to her reading of his paper on the unconscious: "I am always particularly impressed when I read what you have to say on one of my papers. I know that in writing I have to blind myself artificially in order to focus all the light on one dark spot, renouncing cohesion, harmony, rhetoric and everything you call symbolic, frightened as I am by the experience that any such claim or expectation involves the danger of distorting the matter under investigation even though it may embellish it".[14]

Freud, by resisting any but cautionary last words about unifying his theory, appears to Lou to be an obscure figure on a distant horizon, something like Newton's God, the stimulus of the world who sets the machine into motion without giving it direction. Her actual image is more subtle and charming: "This way of acquiring the content of your work has almost too great an attraction... something like looking for eggs in the garden at Easter. One keeps on finding a new egg, which one has perhaps already foolishly passed by several times, and at the same time one sees the Easter bunny in the background laying more eggs."[15] It is often unclear from images like this in Lou's letters whether she thought Freud was playing some kind of game with her, and by extension, everyone else who hung on his words, keeping his own counsel about unifying his work, or whether he truly meant he had nothing but cautionary last words to speak. In any event, she continued to respond to his thought as to a calling to think his ideas through, coordinate them, make his work complete.

Jung and Adler seemed convinced he was playing a power game with them. Surely Freud knew that everything in psychoanalytic theory had to be aimed at a final unifying word? What else justifies the work of psychoanalytic theorizing but the production of a radical system of thought that would change everything? Their perception of the fragmented condition of Freud's work led them to become the feature players in the open rebellion against Freud which resulted in the by now twice-told story of the bloodletting in the Psychoanalytic Association. Freud's response to them was an unwavering resistance to unifying his work. As ambitious as Freud was, he would not compete with them on the ground of their own ambition to complete his work. Instead, they became objects, as did so many others, for the dark side of Freud's style of leadership characterized by Roustang as "dire mastery". Their sin, for Freud, was not so much that they read his work from a scene of completing it, which almost everyone was goaded into doing by its fragmented state, but that they did not show the grace, as so many did, to return their completed version of his work to him as a kind of gift which he could then treat, as he so often did, with either scorn or indifference as it pleased him.

At the end of Freud's work we seem to have what we had at the beginning and throughout its evolution: a work which seems to contest its own coherency. Holt's paper, "On Reading Freud", seems to sum up what Freud's work requires of its readers.[16] The "Decalogue for the Reader of Freud", which ends his paper, commands us to read Freud's work virtuously by neither taking it in vain nor expecting it to synthesize its contradictions. It is certainly true that it is difficult to find synthesizing attempts in Freud's work. His propensity to review the status of his concepts at different points does not clarify things because it also provides the occasion for a movement forward which leaves behind an apparent legacy of further inconsistencies and ambiguities. In "The Ego and the Id", for example, Freud finally identifies ego as the kind of agency so important to contemporary psychoanalytic theorizing. This identification, however, serves as a basis for pushing ahead into the dark and uncertain speculations already established in "Beyond the Pleasure Principle". As a result, reading Freud's work never seems to call for exegetically uncovering hidden meanings, but for conferring meaning by transposing it onto a new ground as part of a project to complete it by revising it.

We can see more clearly the frustration that goads revisionist readings if we shift the emphasis on the incoherency read into Freud's work from its content - its failure to coordinate its different topics, the clinical, the metapsychological, the sociocultural - to its failure to meet the formal requirements for a coherent narrative. The representation of reality by theory requires a narrative form, as Hayden White has shown, whether or not we see merit, as does White, in questioning how that form has epistemological consequences for the content of the theory.[17] Narrative assumes a coherent form when it describes its events as aiming toward an end which will cast its "light back over the events originally recorded in order to redistribute the force of a meaning that was imminent in all of the events from the beginning."[18] Freud's work leaves its readers hard pressed to know where it is meant to go. With inconsistency, contradiction and hyperbole surrounding its concepts it gives the appearance of a mystery story whose readers find it difficult to follow because they cannot anticipate the closure which will give it a unified meaning. In other words, Freud's work consistently seems to give its readers a sense of going somewhere, while consistently seeming to contest the rules of a coherent theoretical narrative which makes the world speak "itself as a story".[19] Attributing this kind of failure to Freud's work puts it perilously close to refusing meaning itself. The project of reading Freud's work to complete it does not mean adding to or elaborating meaning that is already there, or guiding an already coherent plot more steadily and consistently to an end it already aims at, but rather positing an end it lacks to reorganize it into a coherently unified work.

In revisionist readings of Freud, this end is given a particular kind of content dictated by assumptions read into the fact that psychoanalytic theory and psychoanalytic therapy are inseparable. Freud's theory never loses touch with its starting point as a "codification of what takes place in the analytic situation, and more precisely in the analytic relationship".[20] His concept of therapy is informed by the idea of thinking as a reflective work of consciousness directed toward its own thoughts. Freud shares a common ground with the starting point, stated by Smith, for a philosophy of mind: "To think is to represent. All thought is by a subject and of something. In broadest usage what we mean by thinking is coextensive with what we mean by mind and the realm of the psychological."[21] Needless to say, a host of philosophical conundrums follow from this starting point, and Freud has something to say about many of them, but, typically, not in a synthesized form. Instead he insists on an interdependency between theory and therapy which orphans psychoanalysis from the contemplative character of philosophical thought. For instance, while he admits that some of his ideas can be found in Schopenhauer and Nietzsche, he claims never to have read them, something, with respect to the latter at least, we have every reason to doubt. Similarly he never refers to Husserl, who was not only his contemporary, but who, like him, had studied under Brentano. Freud gives us no help in finding our way through his theory except in "its double aspect of being both a method of investigation and of therapeutic treatment".[22]

Freud gives his idea of a self-reflective work of consciousness a distinctive psychoanalytic mark: What defines consciousness as such a work is its opposition to another work, a work that goes on in the region of the unconscious mind. Freud invents psychoanalytic therapy by defining a precondition for the self's work of consciousness: The self must first degrade its sense of power over its thoughts by identifying thinking as a work that is also an unconscious work. The term "unconscious" has a history that precedes Freud - "at least six books were published during the 1870s with the word 'unconscious' in their titles".[23] But it is Freud who made the concept his own by not referring to the unconscious as a site that doubles the site of consciousness. Freud's concept dissolved the rationalist view which assigns the unconscious, to quote Archaud, "exactly those characteristics of the conscious mind, namely ideas, desires, beliefs, etc. excepting the fact that these latter are, in the case of 'the unconscious', ones of which the individual is unaware".[24] The rationalist views the idea of the unconscious as acceptable only when it is the inferior term to consciousness. Freud's brief against Janet's theory of Hysteria, was directed precisely against this view. Freud rejected Janet's notion that to understand Hysteria we must start by identifying what is human with the "field of consciousness". He rejected the definition of Hysteria as an "abnormal restriction of that field" marked by a loss of the "normal mental activity that presupposes a certain capacity for 'synthesis', the ability to unite several ideas into a complex... to apperceive impressions from the other senses - i.e. to take them up into...conscious thought".[25] Janet does not stress, but neither does he preclude, the existence of unconscious ideas. They exist as a kind of detritus that splits off from consciousness. Consciousness can recover the power of its functions only when it becomes aware that it is present to itself as incomplete.

Freud's concept of "the unconscious" constitutes a radically powerful reversal of the rationalist view. Consciousness is not first in our understanding of the mind, but last. "Let us assume that every mental process exists to begin with in an unconscious stage or phase and that it is only from there that the process passes over into the conscious phase, just as a photographic picture begins as a negative and only becomes a picture after being turned into a positive. Not every negative however, necessarily becomes a positive; nor is it necessary that every unconscious mental process should turn into a conscious one".[26] The self, doing a psychoanalytic work of reflection, must never assume consciousness is the starting point for the development of its mind with the unconscious splitting off later to be dragged behind like a coexisting mind. In Freud we find only one mind with consciousness one of its "attributes" that appears last. Freud enjoins us to make the notion of "the unconscious" refer to the site where the processes of mind first produce ideas. The unconscious is both the site on which exaggerated desires first appear that are in conflict with the world and the site on which processes go on that cannot be associated with conscious processes. This is one of the thrusts of Freud's famous "second" topographical description of the mind which refuses to identify ego with consciousness, while at the same time identifying it with the work of defense, disguise, repression, inhibition, etc. If it is true, as Freud states, that consciousness is the attribute that "forms the point of departure for all our investigations"[27] because "it is the only characteristic of psychic processes that is directly presented to us"[28] it is also true that it tells us little about our psychic processes. "It would put an end to all misunderstandings if, from now on, in describing the various kinds of psychical acts we were to disregard the question of whether they were conscious or unconscious. . ."[29] The self's conscious ideas and beliefs have no significance beyond pointing to spaces and gaps which must be filled in with unconscious ideas and beliefs if they are to become coherent. It is precisely Freud's discovery that a self mediated by the psychoanalytic discourse can itself do this work that invests it with a power over its thinking.

This much is indisputably true for Freud's revisionists, but it is their assumptions about what goes on in the psychoanalytic discourse which dictates the content of an end that must be posited for Freud's theory if it is to be a coherent narrative. These assumptions seem self-evident: Psychoanalytic therapy involves a self struggling to perform a work of consciousness which will liberate it from being imprisoned in distorted desires which interdict vivifying exchanges with the world, producing, in effect, a life that is lifeless. The self in psychoanalytic therapy is alienated from its own experience, lost in a language it speaks but does not understand, enacting desires that are incoherent to it. Psychoanalytic therapy is a technical discourse which introduces a self to its own consciousness as a work by which it can restore itself as the subject of its own possibilities.

What goads revisionist readers of Freud's work to complete it is its failure to define the work of consciousness as a liberating work. It is not technique that can define a liberating work, but what that work aims at that represents human possibility. Revising Freud's theory completes it by positing a vision of human possibility constitutive of the definition of the work of consciousness which allows the theory to function as it was presumably intended to from the beginning: as a guide for a self struggling to realize its possibilities against an unconscious work that threatens to destroy them. Because no such vision can be found in Freud's work, his revisionists read it as a failure to deliver on the promise of consciousness as a liberating work.

The sense of scandal associated with this failure cannot be underestimated as a goad to revisionists. Not only does Freud threaten his own personal claim to greatness, but the contribution psychoanalysis can make in helping humans formulate the meaning of their own suffering. Is it not Freud who shows us, as Mary Rawlinson argues, that "suffering names the experience of and alienation from or disruption in one's own ends or purposive activity and an inability to maintain the ordered wholeness of one's world"?[30] And what can this disruption mean if not separation from a world on which "a horizon of value is inscribed ... shaped by regulative principles such as moral laws, principles of conduct, or styles of character, and given substance by constellations of possibilities invested with concern or taken as ends"?[31] Is not psychoanalysis destined by the very conditions of its origin to be one of the "antagonists of loneliness and isolation (which) always hover, more or less nearly, in the wings"[32] ready to make an entrance on the stage of the world? In a sense, every revision which claims to complete Freud, doubles what it perceives to be Freud's original promise to give us a theory which defines consciousness as a liberating work. Freud may have presented us with the promise of psychoanalysis, but it is the revision which claims to fulfill it by supplying it with a vision of human possibility he resisted speaking from the beginning.

All of the efforts to complete Freud's work that constitute the continuing history of psychoanalytic thought make up a single scene of reading Freud to complete him. While Ludwig Binswanger and Anna Freud, for example, anchor opposite ends of the spectrum of revisionist thought, they read their revisions into Freud's work from the same scene of demanding that its last word be a vision of human possibility. For Binswanger, this was a question of saving Freud from himself. What and how much, Binswanger rhetorically asks, can we expect from a life of creative scientific effort struggling to make a beginning against old prejudices? It is enough to expect it to be inspired by a great idea that gives rise to a scientific work which "combines the unique personal-psychological and cultural-historical conditions that made it possible with the timeless mission it has to accomplish in and for the world, namely the service of Truth. The idea holds the secret of productivity. Its task, to use a profound phrase of Goethe's is none other than to fulfill the divine mission to be productive". [33]

For Binswanger, the idea that Freud pursued to his limits was that of instinctual man - "the scientific concept of homo natura, man as nature".[34] In that pursuit, Freud "worked out the gigantic structure of his technique of unmasking, and became the first to lift the veil from the riddle of the sphinx known as neurosis".[35] Binswanger's mission was to make the self the true subject of psychoanalysis by grounding it in a meaningful philosophical anthropology denied by Freud's great idea.

The notion that he was on a mission is more than figurative. "It was on a September morning of the year 1927" writes Binswanger in his memoirs, "having broken away from the congress of German neurologists and psychiatrists that was meeting in Vienna, I had hastened to Freud in the Semmering, impatient to return at last the unforgettable visit he had paid me at an unhappy time in my life".[36] He intended, of course, more than a social visit, although it was undoubtedly such as well. We can hardly imagine a visit with Freud in which the conversation would not eventually turn to psychoanalysis. This meant, in Binswanger's case, turning "to what, twenty years earlier, had brought us together and, in spite of considerable differences of opinion, had held us together - his lifework, his 'great idea'." Their friendship, which had never failed, was now put to the test. "Using as a concrete clinical example a very severe case of obsessional neurosis that had greatly preoccupied both of us, I raised the question as to how we were to understand the failure of such patients to take the last decisive step of psychoanalytic insight, which the physician expects of them, and instead persist in their misery in defiance of all efforts and technical progress made so far".[37] The question was clearly meant to open a discourse with Freud on what was needed to complete psychoanalysis. Freud had identified those themes that set into play a family drama of conflicting loyalties and punitive superego recriminations without which there could never have been a psychoanalytic therapy. But psychoanalytic therapy was bracketed by a theory that was less a theory than a congeries of fragmented observations. It could be unified only by a principle that envisions the possibilities a human being must realize through his exchanges with the world. Articulating this principle, eventually came to mean for Binswanger, describing human beings in an existential language that has passed through Heidegger to closely resemble the early language of Sartre. Human beings embody the principle of their own possibilities, whatever limits the world itself may place on them, because they are subjects who constitute the meaning of their own being in the world by constituting the meaning of the beings of the world.[38] Binswanger, however, in the Semmering, was raising the specific question of why patients resist taking the last step to liberate themselves. It was 1927, and Freud had not yet pulled his work together around the answer to this vexing question. It was time at last to bring the idea of curing pathology into the province of a coherent psychoanalytic theory. It was not, for Binswanger, a question of Freud's faulty technique, but of his failure to address the question of human possibilities. "Only if we conceive and define the sick person as a human being" he was later to write, "can we recognize and determine in what ways he deviates from the norm of being human, just as biology and neurology can describe the degeneration or deficiency of a normal function only if they have conceived and defined the sick person as an organism".[39] Freud, who had traced "the tangled pathways of the dream, the theories of neuroses, of paranoia, of infantile sexuality and so on. . ."[40] through the psychoanalytic discourse conceptualized as an archaeology of the self, ironically had lost sight of the self by pursuing in the dark a vague outline of a biology of the instincts and the mental apparatus it supplied with energy.

Binswanger thought that Freud was lost because he felt he had "little need of philosophy".[41] In 1913 he had visited Freud with his philosopher friend, Paul Haberlin. Haberlin remembered how inadequately Freud had answered questions about the logic of his theory, and how inadequate his knowledge of Kant had been. One of Haberlin's memories is particularly telling: "Freud said - but not quite seriously, it seemed to me - that philosophy was one of the most respectable forms of the sublimation of repressed sexuality, nothing more. I countered with the question, What then is science, and psychoanalytic psychology in particular? Thereupon, visibly somewhat surprised, he said evasively: 'At least psychology has social usefulness'".[42] Binswanger's questioning of Freud on his 1927 visit carries something of the same thrust of Haberlin's question. Like Haberlin, Binswanger was not questioning Freud to reprimand Freud for his failure, but to begin to save him from himself.

Binswanger's contribution to the salvation of Freud lay in his suggestion that a patient's failure "might be understood as the result of something that could only be called a 'deficiency of spirit', that is, an inability on the part of the patient to raise himself to the level of 'spiritual communication' with the physician." Freud's response so surprises Binswanger that he recalls "I could hardly believe my ears". "Yes," Freud responds, "spirit is everything. . .Mankind has always known that it possesses spirit; I had to show that there are also instincts. But men are always unsatisfied, they cannot wait, they always want something whole and ready made; but one has to begin somewhere and only very slowly move forward." Binswanger is not ready to hear this as a cautionary last word. Instead, he hears an admission that encourages him to pursue his own last word. He thinks he heard the basis for an agreement toward which he presses: "I went a step further," Binswanger reports, "explaining that I found myself forced to recognize in man something like a basic religious category; that in any case it was impossible for me to admit that 'the religious' was a phenomenon that could somehow be derived from something else." Binswanger then adds parenthetically that he had been thinking of "something that I have since learned to call the religious I-thou relationship". But he had "stretched the bow of agreement too far and began to feel its resistance". Freud reaches into his desk and shows Binswanger his recently completed manuscript on "The Future of an Illusion". The interview is over. "Freud walked with me to the door. His last words, spoken with a shrewd slightly ironic smile, were: 'I am sorry I cannot satisfy your religious needs'". [43]

Binswanger's Freud is a Freud whose last word failed what psychoanalytic theory needs to define a work of consciousness as a liberating power: a vision of human possibility that defines what it is to be human. Binswanger, surprised by Freud's first response that spirit is everything, seemed not at all surprised when confronted by "The Future of an Illusion". This was the iconoclastic Freud he expected; the Freud whose surprise at Haberlin's remarks did not lead him to beat a retreat from his own illogical rejection of philosophy as a synthesizing discipline of thought, but rather, to reaffirm it with a weak parry to Haberlin's thrust. This was the Freud who, showing Binswanger at the end a smile like the Cheshire cat, at times turned his own failed last words on his own invention, calling his metapsychology his "witch", his theory of instincts his "mythology", and stating as early as 1907 that "our understanding reaches as far as our anthropomorphism".[44] This was also the Freud who was never willing to let himself be saved from himself.

Anna doubles Binswanger's project of saving Freud. Sharing her father's disdain for dealing with philosophical ideas, her tone for completing Freud's work is more practical than Binswanger's. In Anna's scene of completing Freud she does not confront Freud's failures, but those of his inheritors. She reprimands them for assuming that it is an "apostasy from psychoanalysis as a whole" to deflect research "from the id to the ego".[45] The idea that animated Freud's investigations concerned "infantile phantasies carried on into adult life, imaginary gratifications and the punishments apprehended in retribution for these".[46] The problem is, that "somehow or another, many analysts had conceived the idea that, in analysis, the value of the scientific and therapeutic work done was in direct proportion to the depth of the psychic strata upon which attention was focused".[47] The term "many analysts" must include Freud himself. But he was the beginning, and deficiencies in beginnings are forgivable. It is now time to turn to what was implicit though unspoken in Freud's theory - "that the proper field for our observation is always the ego".[48] It is time, in effect, for psychoanalysis to fulfill its promise as a therapy by grounding its theory in the relationship between the dynamics that shape the self's inner world and its adaptation to the demands of the outer world in which its possibilities lie. Achieving the virtues of health can be realized only by a theory that centers itself on the autonomous institutions of the ego. This is another way of saying that if psychoanalysis is to be a healing process, it must be given a vision of human possibility to define the work of consciousness as a liberating work. Freud must be saved by saving him from others who cannot read precisely that intention in his incomplete theory.

Anna's project is to bring to bear the investigations of "infantile phantasies carried on into adult life, imaginary gratifications and the punishments apprehended in retribution for these" on "problems such as that of children or adults to the outside world". What psychoanalysis is missing are "concepts of value, such as health and disease, virtue or vice ..."[49] Anna is the one who knows that Freud knew that psychoanalysis could not be defined as a psychology of the unconscious, for such a "definition immediately loses all claim to accuracy when we apply it to psychoanalytic therapy".[50] She knows that Freud himself pointed to the direction in which to complete his work: "to the study of the ego...to explore its contents, its boundaries and its functions and to trace the influences in the outside world, the id and the superego by which it has been shaped and, in relation to the id, to give an account of the instincts..."[51] Anna's language is a far cry from Binswanger's. She hews closely to the dry passionless language of the objective scientific observer. Both, however, read Freud from the same scene of completing him: Freud's theory, born as a codification of the therapeutic discourse, fails to develop a vision of human possibility in relation to which we can read the alignment of human purposes. For Anna, our knowledge of ego supplies that vision. Once we know the ego, we save psychoanalysis: "The investigation of the id and of its mode of operation was always only a means to an end. And the end was invariably the same: the correction of...abnormalities and the restoration of the ego to its integrity".[52] Like Binswanger, Anna claims that completing Freud means revising his insistence on the explanatory power of his doctrine of the instincts, couched in terms of a chimerical metapsychology. This insistence consumed him, deflecting him from investigating the developmental history of the self as a teleological movement toward its possibilities. Defining this movement in terms of a vision of human possibility that is the end it aims toward, measures the pathological deviations to be rectified by a work of consciousness. Completing Freud means leaving him behind in order to carry forward the power of consciousness to leave behind the unconscious forces which betray the self forcing it to betray its own possibilities.

*

On the face of it, the assumption that sets the revisionist scene of reading Freud seems to be straightforward enough: While Freud never loses sight of the self struggling to realize its possibilities, he loses sight of the struggling self as the subject of psychoanalytic theory. Freud the father, wills five conditions with the legacy of psychoanalysis: resistance, repression, the unconscious, the etiological significance of sexual life and the importance of infantile experiences.[53] They are his testament, setting the direction for psychoanalytic theorizing toward further study of the forces which lie below the surface of the self shaping its experiences. While this direction is the *sine qua non* of psychoanalytic theorizing, Freud never finds his way back to the surface where the self interacts with its world and the work of consciousness that justifies psychoanalysis can be defined. Ryecroft alludes to this in the case of the dream which Freud willed to psychoanalysis as its emblem. Freud brought dreams into the province of meaningful human activity by approaching them not as "phenomena we observe but experiences we have and create for ourselves."[54] But his approach was flawed precisely because he lost sight of them as a creation of the self. As a result, he obliterated "the distinction between health and illness. If dreams are both universally occurring experiences and abnormal psychic phenomena, then the healthy are virtual neurotics, and the distinction between health and wholeness on the one hand and illness and lack of integration on the other goes by the board ... If, as Freud agreed, there is some connection between dreams and the waking imagination ... (then) works of art which are humanly admired for their beauty and truth become scientifically only explicable in terms implying pathology, thereby conflating admiration and disparagement, excellence and illness."[55] Freud's theoretical journey, in effect, from the "Interpretation of Dreams" to "Leonardo" marks him with the irony of appearing like the ego he once described as "walking in a country which he does not know..."[56] Immersed in analyzing how the self struggles to protect itself with cunning defenses whose prototype is the dream work, Freud loses sight of the self working to realize its own possibilities. He becomes lost, as it were, in a theory which contests its completion with a vision of human possibility.

Yet precisely because it is a theory which contests its completion, the assumption that the self is its subject must be put into question. Paul Ricoeur, in a close reading of Freud's work which, although part of his own revisionist project to restore the self as the subject of psychoanalytic theory, shows us, nevertheless, that when we allow it, Freud's theory gives us its subject in its own terms. The direction which Freud's theorizing takes, from beginning to end, Ricouer points out, makes his work "a mixed discourse. It intermingles questions of meaning (the meaning of dreams, symptoms, culture, etc.) and questions of force (cathexis, economic accounting, conflict, repression, etc.)... this mixed discourse is not equivocal but is appropriate to the reality which it wishes to take into account, namely the binding of force and meaning in a semantics of desire".[57] Returning to the dream which Ricoeur notes is "not only the first object of his investigation but a model ... of all the disguised, substitutive, and fictive expressions of human wishing or desire, Freud invites us to look to dreams themselves for the various relations between dreams and language. First, it is not the dream as dreamed that can be interpreted, but rather the text of the dream account; analysis attempts to substitute for this text another text the primitive speech of desire ... This semantics of desire relates to the dynamics expressed in the notions of discharge, repression, cathexis, etc. But it is important to stress from the start that this dynamics - or energetics, or even hydraulics - is articulated only in a semantics: the 'vicissitudes of instincts', to use one of Freud's expressions, can be attained only in the vicissitudes of meaning ... All ... psychical productions belong to the area of meaning and come under a unified question: How do desires achieve speech? How do desires make speech fail, and why do they themselves fail to speak?"[58]

The heart of Freud's work could not be stated more clearly. Bracketing how Ricouer transposes Freud's work onto his own ground, the subject of Freud's theory, taken in its own terms, also could not be stated more clearly: Its subject is the meaning of desire, defined in the first instance as the painful experience of an absence that impels us toward the objects of the world signified as the absent, and in the second instance, an experience of absence that is not a primordial lack, but a signifier of the presence of the fullness of an energic force called the instincts. "When (Freud) speaks to us of instincts, he speaks of them in and from the level of expression, that is, in and from certain effects of meaning which give themselves to be deciphered and can be treated as texts..."[59] By insisting that Freud's theory, "at times states conflicts of force subject to an energetics, at times relations of meaning subject to a hermeneutics",[60] Ricouer is insisting that it must be read as presenting us with an aporia - a conceptual impasse in which the interpreted symbol is defined by two perspectives, each of which demands that we see the other as an error: the symbol is a coded message that signifies intentions, but the intentions it signifies are those of mindless natural forces and energies called "instincts". Put another way, if every interpretation of meaning needs a frame of reference for its starting point, then the interpretation of the meaning of desire in Freud, has instincts as its frame - "an intentionality" as Needleman has put it, "in which no essential reference is made to an agent-self".[61]

Yet even when interpreting the meaning of desire in terms of an aporia, Freud cannot lose sight of the problem of defining consciousness as a work. Consciousness cannot be made to disappear as an intentional work or the justification for psychoanalysis itself disappears. "The fact of being conscious" Ricoeur reminds us, "can be neither suppressed nor destroyed. For it is in relation to the possibility of becoming conscious, in relation to the task of achieving conscious insight, that the concept of a psychical representative of an instinct becomes meaningful."[62]

Freud never seriously addresses the question of what kind of "fact" is "being conscious". Binswanger's friend, Haberlin, heard in Freud's general attack on philosophy and specific ignorance of Kant, an unfortunate avoidance of this question. What Haberlin did not seem to appreciate, for whatever reason, is that Freud's lack of interest in the ontological definition of consciousness, the consuming interest in Western Philosophy, was counterbalanced by a consuming interest in the possibility of becoming conscious - i.e., in the question of the efficacy of consciousness as a work opposed to the work of the unconscious. Freud is drawn into the question by the fact that every patient resists the very treatment he seeks. It is this resistance which, Laplanche and Pontalis point out, "may be said to have played a decisive part in the foundation of psychoanalysis. In fact hypnosis and suggestion were rejected essentially because the passive resistance that certain patients set up against them seemed to Freud at once legitimate and impossible to overcome or to interpret by such methods."[63] As central as the fact of resistance is to defining the technique of psychoanalytic practice, revisionists have pushed resistance to the margins of its theory. Freud, after all, did tell us that each of the agencies of the mind are a source of resistance.[64] Isn't this another way of saying the self is always "reason enough for the resistance",[65] and reason enough for the self to transcend it with the help and guidance of the analyst? But if for revisionists, "resistance" lies at the margins of psychoanalytic theory, in Freud's work it moves to the center, resulting in the frustration and confusion presented by one of Freud's last great texts, "Analysis Terminable and Interminable".

Sometimes misread as a paper dealing with the "theory of technique"[66] in which Freud "offers a systematic examination of the process of analysis",[67] "Analysis Terminable and Interminable" is a long paper comprising eight sections. Through section four, Freud offers a soothing balm about the difficulties encountered in psychoanalytic therapy. He gives us a tour through arguments about the way the strength of the instincts impose difficulties on producing desirable modifications of the ego. Along the way he expresses the hope that "metapsychological speculation. . ."[68] can eventually produce a kind of algorithm for solving the conflict between the ego and the id. Section five begins a reversal of that hope. He introduces something new, like a wild card, into the deliberations. It is bad enough that the "normal ego. . ., like normality in general, (is) an ideal fiction"[69] but the analyst who must try "to explain to the patient... the distortions which his defense has produced and to correct it. . ." must see "that there *is* a resistance against the uncovering of resistances and that the defensive mechanisms really do deserve the name which we gave them originally before they had been more closely examined. They are resistances not only to the making conscious of contents of the id, but also to analysis as a whole, and thus to recovery". [70]

He is finally answering Binswanger's question about why patients will not take the last step toward their cure, but instead repeat their illness made visible in the scene of the transference. When all is said and done, resistance to the uncovering of resistances eludes explanation in terms of impoverished theoretical thinking or unrefined techniques. As Glover puts it in the technical language of the practicing analyst, "having exhausted the possibilities of resistance arising from the ego or the superego, we are faced with the bare fact that a set of presentations is being repeated before us again and again ... We expected that by removing the ego and superego resistances we should bring about something like automatic release of pressure, that the charge would either dissipate itself explosively and openly, or that some other manifestation of defence would immediately arise to bind the freed energy, as happens in transitory symptom formation. Instead we seem to have given a fillip to the repetition compulsion, and the id has made use of weakened ego defenses to exercise an increased attraction on preconscious presentations." [71]

The possibility of that perplexing and vexing "fillip" to which Glover refers means for Freud that resistance is an effect of the instincts. The "fact" of resistance, Freud tells us, leads to the Empedoclian principle that informs "Beyond the Pleasure Principle", his darkest speculations about the instincts: "The two fundamental principles of Empedocles... are, both in name and in function, the same as our two primal instincts, Eros and Destructiveness..." [72]

In "Analysis Terminable and Interminable" Freud joins repetition to resistance, while separating both from the idea of an agent-self. He refuses to allow psychoanalytic therapy to be conceived of as a linear movement, no matter how erratic its course, which features a self that leaves its conflicts behind. Instead, he underscores in the clinical setting what he has already formulated in his socio-cultural texts: nothing is ever left behind. Almost at the end of the paper, he offers a solace to psychoanalysts: "Here let us pause for a moment to assure the analyst that he has our sincere sympathy in the very exacting demands he has to fulfill in carrying out his activities. It almost looks as if analysis were the third of those 'impossible' professions in which one can be sure beforehand of achieving unsatisfying results. The other two, which have been known much longer, are education and government."[73] This constitutes no less than a triad of impossibilities that renders a psychoanalytic vision of human possibilities impossible.

At the end of "Analysis Terminable and Interminable", in place of a work of consciousness guided by a vision of human possibility, Freud leaves us with the only definition of a work of consciousness we ever find in his theory: a work of suspicion whose efficacy now finds its limits by putting under the sign of suspicion the meaning of the self's struggles to leave its conflicts behind. As Binswanger and Anna exemplify, Freud's revisionists want this ending to represent an incompleteness which calls for a normative theory of the self's relationship to the world. This points to the necessity of giving Freud's theory a starting point other than its own; a starting point fashioned by linking psychoanalytic theorizing to other disciplines whose theorizing concerns envisioning social life as the scene in which humans can realize their possibilities.

Freud's cultural texts are not ancillary to the evolution of his work, but imminent in it. The projects of Marcuse, Fromm and Rieff, to cite three of the most prominent contemporary figures who have woven different strands of political thought into the history of psychoanalytic thought, recognize this. Their differences are less important than the fact that each knows that it is value which constructs the world, and that the starting point for a psychoanalysis that takes the self as its subject must be a world constructed by value that shapes the experiences of the self and as a result can save it. Even Rieff, for example, who recognizes that Freud's work contains no theory of value, formulates the project of reading into it "lessons on the right conduct of life..."[74] Rieff completes Freud with a last word composed out of a blend of history and sociology suffused with an existential coloring. It is culture that supplies human beings with a sense of coherent purposes "for the control of panic and the filling up of emptiness".[75] Freud was swept into prominence less because of anything he said about human behavior, than because he was a dominating figure contributing to a historical disintegration of old compelling beliefs upon which men once depended. No use crying over spilt milk. Once dead, old beliefs cannot be resuscitated. It is the way of history. What remains is to complete Freud, the great iconoclast, by finding the values in his iconoclasm that can define human possibility and guide the work of consciousness in establishing new coherent purposes that bind humans to a new culture in a new age. For Rieff, Marcuse, and Fromm, Freud was a visionary without knowing it because he did not understand history and sociology, or, for that matter, human suffering, as they understand it. It is only when psychoanalytic theory is linked to a theory about the world as its starting point, can the world be moved into the clinic to give the self a vision of its possibilites to love in place of a love that alienates it.

For this is what value represents, a vision to love that is privileged from suspicion because it represents human possibility. Binswanger, for example, argues with Freud that love must be conceived of as a primordial force, above suspicion, and that psychoanalytic theory can be completed only when love is given something to love. But for Freud, resistance is the sign which refuses to put aside the question of the desires which love conceals by conflating desire and love into the struggles of a self to realize its possibilities. In Freud, love is never primordial but a derivative of a desire whose meaning must be interpreted in terms of the purposes pursued by the instincts.

By calling for the meaning of love to be put under the sign of suspicion, Freud moves the transference into the world as the world. "The Future of an Illusion", Freud's last word to Binswanger at their 1927 meeting, does indeed read as a polemic delivered against the superstition of religion by a son of the Enlightenment. Perhaps this is why Freud, who was conflicted enough over being consigned an historical identity to destroy parts of his correspondence came to dislike it enough to call it "childish ... weak analytically and inadequate as a self confession". The concept of "resistance" haunts "The Future of an Illusion" to the point to which Freud virtually rewrote it in "Civilization and Its Discontents" which, as we shall see later, features resistance as its main theoretical problem. Nevertheless, beneath the patina of its rationalism, "The Future of an Illusion" depicts repeated appeals for a healing love as the unsurpassable structure of the world just as the repetition of that selfsame illusion structures the scene of the transference which resists dissolution.

Freud's efforts to formulate a language in which to speak about the instincts results in the construction of a mythology. The mythological language of instincts governs the texts on culture that form the last part of his work, although Freud is always telling us how uncomfortably conflicted he is over their speculative content. At the same time, quoting Freud, "if we cannot see clearly at least we see the obscurities clearly", Hyman points out he is inordinately fond of using throughout his work "an oxymoron, illuminated darkness".[76] The obscurities which we can see clearly only in the dark are, in the last analysis, the instincts. And the instincts are troped in the mythological language that governs the last part of his work as the darkness which illuminates the meaning of the human world of meaning.

Freud's metaphor for instincts as a darkness that illuminates appears at the beginning of his work and dominates it at the end. The theoretical Chapter Seven in "The Interpretation of Dreams" opens with the statement: "Unless I am greatly mistaken, all the paths along which we have travelled have led us towards the light - towards elucidation and fuller understanding." Making sense of dreams tells us about the exaggerated wishes in the unconscious and about the work which the unconscious does to disguise them. "But as soon as we endeavor to penetrate more deeply into the mental process involved in dreaming, every path will end in darkness. There is no possibility of explaining dreams as a psychical process, since to explain a thing means to trace it back to something already known, and there is at the present time no established psychological knowledge under which we could subsume what the psychological examination of dreams enables us to infer as a basis for their explanation. On the contrary, we shall be obliged to set up a number of fresh hypotheses which touch tentatively upon the structure of the apparatus of the mind and upon the play of forces operating in it." He ends the chapter with an honest admission that the dark region that can never be illuminated but without which there can be no illumination is the home of psychoanalysis: "It may well be that this first portion of our psychological study of dreams will leave us with a sense of dissatisfaction. But we can console ourselves with the thought that we have been obliged to build our way out into the dark. If we are not wholly in error, other lines of approach are bound to lead us into much the same region and the time may then come when we shall find ourselves more at home in it." [77]

Mixing light and dark is Freud's recipe for psychoanalytic theorizing throughout his work. In the end we are not all that far from where we were at the beginning. In the last paper published in his lifetime, "Constructions in Analysis", Freud returns to one of his favorite analogies, the similarity between archaeology and psychoanalysis. Following the pattern of his discursive style, he first sounds a note of optimism: "The analyst. . .works under more favorable conditions than the archaeologist since he has at his disposal material which can have no counterparts in excavations, such as the repetition of reactions dating from infancy and all that emerges in connection with these repetitions through the transference. . .the excavator is dealing with destroyed objects. . .But it is different with the psychical object whose early history the analyst is seeking to recover." Then comes the pessimistic note. "There are only two other facts that weigh against the extraordinary advantage which is thus enjoyed by the work of analysis: namely, that psychical objects are incomparably more complicated than the excavator's material ones and that we have insufficient knowledge of what we may expect to find, since their finer structure contains so much that is still mysterious." And finally the last word to the effect that psychoanalysis will always find itself building out into a darkness that illuminates: "For the archaeologist the reconstruction is the aim and end of his endeavors while for analysis the construction is only a preliminary labor."[78] It is a labor which can only go on groping in the dark where myths live.

Freud's mythological language of the instincts is the means by which he moves his work toward an end which supplies it with the coherency of a unified narrative. It is an end which justifies psychoanalysis itself by defining a work of consciousness as a work that opposes the unconscious work of constructing a world out of loving visions of human possibility. This end is haunted by the scandal of calling consciousness to a work of placing our love of a healing love under a sign of suspicion as we would a symptom. This end is not a unifying last word that proved easy for Freud to speak. Psychoanalysis, after all, left without a last word, may not be much to love, but can it be loved at all if its last word opposes love? Nevertheless, Freud's last cultural texts which many revisionists regard as his most fragmented and incoherent, riddled as they are with his own apologetic language, lead his work into the twentieth century precisely because they point to an end that defines the work of consciousness in terms of putting love under the sign of suspicion.

If we are to follow Freud's work to this end we must follow it through a series of reversals which turn the revisionist narrative about the meaning of the transference against itself.

References

1 Vincent Brome, *Freud and His Early Circle*, New York, William Morrow, 1968, p. 21.

2 Paul Roazen, *Freud and His Followers*, New York, New York University Press, 1984, p. 214.

3 Patrick Mahony, *Freud as a Writer*, New York, International Universities Press, 1982, p. 204.

4 Patrick Mahony, *Cries of the Wolf Man*, New York, International Universities Press, 1984, p. 98 fn.

5 Mahony, 1982, p. 15.

6 J. Laplanche and J.-B. Pontalis, *The Language of Psychoanalysis*, tr. Donald Nicholson-Smith, New York, W. W. Norton, 1973, p. vii.

7 Ibid., p. xii - xiii.

8 Francois Roustang, *Dire Mastery*, tr. Ned Lukacher, Baltimore, The Johns Hopkins University Press, 1982, p.66.

9 Ibid., p. 65.

10 Ernst Pfeiffer, ed. *Sigmund Freud and Lou Andreas-Salome: Letters*, tr. William and Elaine Robson-Scott, London, Hogarth, 1972, p. 32.

11 Ibid., p. 106

12 Ibid., p. 81.

13 Norman O. Brown, *Life Against Death*, New York, Vintage Books, 1959, Chapter IX.

14 Ernst Pfeiffer, ed. 1972, p.45.

15 Ibid., p.48.

16 Robert R. Holt, "On Reading Freud", in Carrie Lee Rothgeb, ed. *Abstracts of the Standard Edition of the Complete Psychological Works of Sigmund Freud*, New York, Jason Aronson, 1973.

17 Hayden White, *The Content of the Form*, Baltimore, The Johns Hopkins University Press, 1987, p. ix.

18 Ibid., p. 20.

19 Ibid., p. 2.

20 Paul Ricoeur, "The Question of Proof in Freud's Psychoanalytic Writings" in Charles E. Reagen and David Stewart, eds. *The Philosophy of Paul Ricoeur*, Boston, Beacon Press, 1978, p. 185.

21 Joseph H. Smith, ed., *Thought, Consciousness, and Reality*, New Haven, Yale University Press, 1977, p. x.

22 Paul Ricoeur, 1978, p. 184.

23 David Archard, *Consciousness and the Unconscious*, Lasalle, Illinois, Open Court, 1984, p. 14.

24 Ibid., p. 16.

25 Sigmund Freud and Joseph Breuer, *Studies on Hysteria*, tr. James Strachey, New York, Discus/Avon, 1966, p. 142; 274.

26 Sigmund Freud, *The Complete Introductory Lectures on Psychoanalysis*, tr. James Strachey, New York, W.W. Norton, 1966, p. 295.

27 Sigmund Freud, "The Unconscious", *Standard Edition*, V. 14: p. 172.

28 Ibid., p.192.

29 Ibid., p. 172.

30 Mary C. Rawlinson, "The Sense of Suffering", *The Journal of Medicine and Philosophy*, 11: 1, Feb. 1986, p. 50.

31 Ibid., p. 48.

32 Ibid., p. 45.

33 Ludwig Binswanger, *Being-in-the-World: Selected Papers*, tr with intro, Jacob Needleman, New York, Harper Torchbooks, 1968, p. 149-150.

34 Ibid., p. 150.

35 Ibid., p. 151.

36 Ibid., p. 182.

37 Ibid., p. 182.

38 Jacob Needleman, "A Critical Introduction to Ludwig Binswanger's Existential Psychoanalysis" in Ludwig Binswanger, 1968, Ch. VI.

39 Gerald N. Izenberg, *The Existentialist Critique of Freud*, Princeton, Princeton University Press, 1976, p. 219-220.

40 Ludwig Binswanger, *Sigmund Freud: Reminiscences of a Friendship*, tr. Norbert Guterman, New York, Grune and Stratton, 1957, p. 3.

41 Ibid., p. 8.

42 Ibid., p. 9.

43 Ludwig Binswanger, 1968, p. 183.

44 quoted in Mahony, 1982, p. 201-202.

45 Anna Freud, *The Ego and the Mechanisms of Defense*, tr. Cecil Baines, New York, International Universities Press, 1946, p. 3.

46 Ibid., p. 3-4.

47 Ibid., p. 3.

48 Ibid., p. 6.

49 Ibid., p. 3-4.

50 Ibid., p. 4.

51 Ibid., p. 4-5.

52 Ibid., p. 4.

53 Sigmund Freud, *An Autobiographical Study*, tr. James Strachey, New York, W. W. Norton, 1952, p. 67.

54 Charles Rycroft, *The Innocence of Dreams*, New York, Pantheon, 1979, p. 2.

55 Ibid., p. 4-5.

56 Sigmund Freud, "Analysis Terminable and Interminable", *Standard Edition*, V. 23: p. 237.

57 Paul Ricoeur, "A Philosophical Interpretation of Freud", in Reagan and Stewart, eds., 1978 p. 169.

58 Paul Ricoeur, *Freud and Philosophy*, tr. Denis Savage, New Haven, Yale University Press, 1970, p. 56.

59 Paul Ricoeur, 1978, p. 172.

60 Paul Ricoeur, 1970, p. 65.

61 Jacob Needleman, 1968, p. 53.

62 Paul Ricoeur, 1970, p. 430.

63 Laplanche and Pontalis, 1973, p. 394-395.

64 Sigmund Freud, *Inhibitions, Symptoms, and Anxiety*, Standard Edition, 26: Part XI.

65 Stanley A. Leavy, "John Keat's Psychology of Creative Imagination", *The Psychoanalytic Quarterly*, 28 (1970): p. 178.

66 Reuben Fine, *Freud: A Critical Evaluation of His Theories*, New York, David McKay, 1962, p. 103.

67 Ibid., p. 237.

68 Sigmund Freud, "Analysis Terminable and Interminable", p. 235.

69 Ibid., p. 235.

70 Ibid., p. 239.

71 Quoted in Laplanche and Pontalis, 1973, p. 396 fn.

72 Sigmund Freud, "Analysis Terminable and Interminable" p. 246.

73 Ibid., p. 248.

74 Philip Rieff, *Freud: The Mind of the Moralist*, Garden City, Doubleday, 1961, p. xix.

75 Philip Rieff, *The Triumph of the Therapeutic*, New York, Harper and Row, 1966, p. 3-4.

76 Stanley Edgar Hyman, *The Tangled Bank*, New York, Atheneum, 1962, p. 404.

77 Sigmund Freud, *The Interpretation of Dreams*, tr. James Strachey, New York, Basic Books, 1955, p. 511.

78 Sigmund Freud, "Constructions in Analysis", *Standard Edition*, V. 23: p. 259.

Part Two

Reversals

Freud actually worked with the patient in only three of his five case studies - Dora, the Rat Man, and the Wolf Man. Contemporary psychoanalytic revisionists tend to judge all three as therapeutic failures because in each, as Mahony puts it, he failed to reach a "stable mature understanding of the transference".[1] Each case poses different therapeutic problems, and represents a different stage in the evolution of Freud's technical appreciation of the transference as the scene of therapeutic action. The case of Dora is the earliest and the one in which Freud's appreciation of the significance of the transference is least developed. Laplanche and Pontalis point out that in Dora "numerous turns of phrase reveal that Freud does not look upon the treatment as a whole, in its structure and dynamics, as a transference relationship". Noting that Freud speaks of "transferences" in the plural, they observe that "Freud remarks that these transferences... do not constitute aids to cure except in so far as they are explicated and 'destroyed' one by one".[2] Still very much under the sway of his great innovative idea that by uncovering memories Dora will correct her conscious experience of the history of her desires, Freud sees Dora, in the grip of the transference, acting out "an essential part of her recollections and phantasies instead of reproducing it in the treatment".[3] He felt that the transference was the obstacle that his skill could not surmount which led to the failure of the case.

We can glean from Freud's letters to Fliess, that he wrote the case of Dora under the sway of an ambition to bring his ideas and psychoanalysis on stage with full fanfare.[4] He was bitterly disappointed at the outcome, characterizing Dora's abrupt cessation of treatment after fifteen months, "just when my hopes for a successful termination were at their highest..." as "an unmistakable act of vengeance on her part".[5] It seems clear from Freud's own prefatory remarks to the case, often caustic in tone to his critics, and contrary to his use of the phrase "Fragment of an Analysis" in its title, Freud intended to present a totalized account of Dora's symptoms. The case study was designed to demonstrate the power of psychoanalytic interpretation to order a human history into a coherent narrative that accounted for the origin and meaning of the symptoms being treated. It is Dora's analysis of her own history that is fragmented, Freud points out, not his. Quoting Freud, Marcus observes that "Freud proceeds to specify what it is that is wrong with the stories his patients tell him. The difficulties are in the first instance formal shortcomings of narrative: the connections, 'even the ostensible ones - are for the most part incoherent,' obscured and unclear; 'and the sequence of different events is uncertain.' In short these narratives are disorganized, and the patients are unable to tell a coherent story of their lives".[6] The meaning of Dora's history depends on Freud inserting unconscious meanings into her fragmented story. These meanings are to be the instrument of her cure. The interpretation of Dora's two dreams is virtually the paradigm for the entire therapeutic process. Freud wants Dora to demonstrate the clinical tour de force that by making her own incoherent desires coherent to herself she would leave her past behind, liberating her capacity to love.

The pivotal event which dominates the therapy is Dora's recounting to Freud the backstairs scene in which Herr K., surprising Dora, embraces and kisses her. Marcus observes that it is "a scene that Freud orchestrates with inimitable richness and to which he recurs thematically at a number of junctures with the tact and sense of form that one associates with a classical composer of music [or with Proust, Mann, or Joyce]... It is the scene between her and Herr K. that took place when she was fourteen years old... and acted Freud said as a 'sexual trauma'".[7] Freud, around this scene, seeks to supply Dora with the critical insight that opens up the conundrum of her symptoms. Despite Dora's insistence that she had felt disgust which prompted her to flee Herr K.'s advances, Freud asserts that "this was surely just the situation to call up a distinct feeling of sexual excitement in a girl of fourteen who had never before been approached".[8] Freud could hardly feel anything but certain about this, since he had already grounded the psychoanalytic theory of development in the development of infantile sexuality. He was committed to understanding human development as the representations in the mind of the movement of instinctual forces doomed to founder on the reality principle. Freud was certain, when he was treating Dora, that although knowledge of the vicissitudes of the instincts was still rudimentary, psychoanalysis would derive its ability from such knowledge to connect the life of the infant and child to a patient's symptoms. In Dora's case the transformation was mediated by a mechanism called the "reversal of affect".[9] Dora, Freud insists, by feeling disgust in that scene with Herr K., was "already entirely and completely hysterical".[10]

Freud offers her the insight about her true feelings with a certain amount of tact. "I questioned the patient very cautiously as to whether she knew anything of the physical signs of excitement in a man's body. Her answer, as touching the present, was 'Yes', but as touching the time of the episode, 'I think not'".[11] Freud's tact was not simply for Dora's sake, "but because I was anxious to subject my assumptions to a rigorous test..."[12] Dora insists that she did not know then what she knows now, but she also does not know the source of her present knowledge. Only psychoanalysis knows that source, and therefore psychoanalysis knows both that she knew then and why that knowledge was later disguised as conscious feelings of disgust.[13] If Dora is to be cured, she would have to use the pivotal insight Freud gives her to trace the meaning of Herr K. in the history of her sexual desires back through a chain of associations that would lead to her father and beyond - to Frau K., and therefore, Freud intimates, to her mother.[14] Freud was wagering the future of psychoanalysis on the assumption that "patients' inability to give an ordered history of their life insofar as it coincides with the history of their illness is not merely characteristic of their neurosis. It also possesses great theoretical significance".[15] Revisionists stage their scene of reading Freud to save him from himself on his failure to grasp that significance.

It is a failure to grasp what, on the face of it, is the most banal feature of the transference. It is banal to say that one can see Dora, as well as the Rat Man and the Wolf Man in the scene of their transferences, as figures of passion afflicted with the suffering of love. The transference stages that suffering as the self's distance from the exalted other who is the object of desire. Positioned on the edge of that distance the self measures the degree to which it is a diminished abject being by the obstacles that fill the distance, forcing it into a warlike struggle to reach the fulfillment promised by the object of its desire. What the passionate self resists, as if it were possessed, sealed off from the world by the intensity of its emotions, is paying attention to anything but reaching the object of its desire through the strategies of war.

Freud confesses, "I did not find it easy... to direct the patient's attention to her relations with Herr K".[16] He could not turn the attention of Dora, the bereft lover, away from himself. Freud reports that "she took her revenge on me as she wanted to take her revenge on him, and deserted me as she believed her self to have been deceived and deserted by him".[17] At the end she leaves treatment, having transferred onto Freud, as he sees it, the "cruel impulses and revengeful motives which have already been used in the patient's ordinary life for maintaining her symptoms..."[18] Dora leaves behind a wounded Freud who fifteen months later exacts his famous vengeance on her vengeance by turning her away after she visits him seeking to renew treatment: "I do not know what kind of help she wanted from me, but I promised to forgive her for having deprived me of the satisfaction of affording her a far more radical cure for her troubles".[19] Freud comments that his failure was due to his inability to "succeed in mastering the transference in good time".[20] Indeed, this comment could easily be extended, as many have, to his inability to master his own counter transference.

No doubt, Freud's failure with Dora was due, at least in part, to a deficient technique. But its true cause, for contemporary revisionists who can place the case in the context of his entire work, is a deficient theory which precluded developing a sufficient technique. Few have stated this as clearly as Erik Erikson.

Whatever reason Freud had to refuse resumption of Dora's treatment, his true failure, for Erikson, was not to know what she wanted from him. This failure was a theoretical blindness. "Psychoanalytic enlightenment," Erikson remarks at the beginning of a remarkably rich essay delivered at a meeting of the American Psychoanalytic Association, "has come full cycle and it is not sexuality that remains unmentioned at evening receptions".[21] It is now possible to close the circle if not on Freud's unspoken last word, then at least on the conceptual region in which the last word will be found: the region defined by "our knowledge of human strength". Freud's instinctual doctrine destined him to confuse Dora's sexual problems with the story of human development as a sexual problem. "I wonder," Erikson asks, "how many of us can follow without protest today Freud's asserting that a healthy young girl would, under such circumstances, have considered Mr. K.'s advances 'neither tactless nor offensive?'" Erikson concedes that Dora's "pathological reactions make her... the classical hysteric of her day," but Freud could not get beyond paying attention to her "sexual conflicts" which signified for him that "only her own conflict between love and repugnance could explain the nature of her symptoms".[22]

Which is to say that Freud must have missed the point of the meaning of the scene between Dora and Herr K. on the stairs. Given that the transference meets the commonplace definition of a scene of passion, revisionists do not seem surprised that Freud never featured an extended discussion of the concept. On the other hand, they intimate that by not doing so he misses grasping the crucial point of what it is the self presumably seeks in its passionately intense emotional investment in such strange objects of desire as the psychoanalyst himself. For Freud's revisionists, missing the point is close to missing everything. What the self seeks in its passion is to escape its passion - to leave behind an emotionality which seals it off from the world for an emotionality that opens it to the possibilities of the world. Freud lost sight of the point which he himself introduced into our understanding of passion. The escape from passion which the self seeks is escape from the family drama.

It is in these terms that Erikson unhesitatingly answers Freud's question as to what kind of help Dora wanted from him: She wanted, beyond Freud's insistence "on the psychic reality behind the historical truth... her doctor to be 'truthful' in the therapeutic relation, that is, to keep faith with her on her terms rather than on those of her father or seducer".[23] Freud could not hear that Dora, in the midst of the duplicity of the K.s, her father and her mother, wanted an end not only to the lies which she told to herself, but to the lies around her. She "was concerned not only with the recognition but also with the joint acknowledgment of the historical truth".[24] Freud could not hear what Dora wanted from him because he did not understand that he was treating a "neurosis... rooted in the developmental crisis of adolescence".[25] This was not a failure of technique, but a failure of theory from which Freud would never recover. He would never understand that it is the subject's need to develop character - a structuralized and organized relationship to the world whose internal experiential counterpart of continuity and sameness Erikson calls "identity" - supplies the momentum for the story of human development. Freud's failure with Dora was, in essence, a particular instance of his general failure to understand that the story of development is a story about a self realizing its possibilities unless it is forced by its history to struggle with its history.

While there are other revisionist terms than Erikson's in which Dora's story is told, they tend to tell the same story. What Freud did not know he had discovered in Dora's transference was "a peculiar type of pathological family interaction which made it especially difficult for the teenager to progress past adolescence."[26] Freud, who taught us that development proceeds by the renunciation of wrong objects of desire in the family for right objects outside the family, did not adequately differentiate sexual desire from love. Benedek calls love "the highest developmental achievement of man."[27] Love, like sex, has the attribute of a primordial drive which relates the self to objects as means to ends. We know love by virtue of bonding the self to right objects which are the means to an end which defines human possibility, not in terms of a specific goal to be achieved at a specific time, but in terms of the structure of a fulfilling life that endures over time. Love is a drive which preserves the objects to which it bonds the self, conflating self concern with a concern for others. It is visions of possibility that identify the right objects which differentiate love from passion. To read Freud accurately, Bettelheim insists, is to read that "the sexual drive presses for immediate satisfaction; it neither knows nor cares for the future. Eros and Psyche do."[28] Visions of human possibility complete psychoanalysis with a coherent theory of love because they follow Freud's insight, which he never exploited, that the world is bound together by the force of love.

Freud's work moves in a different direction, exploiting a chilling insight that reverses the objects of the world as the revisionist starting point for understanding human development. This reversal, decentering the self from the story of its own development in accordance with the tenets of Freud's definition of the instincts as an intentionality without reference to an agent-self, moves the transference out of the clinic into the world as the world. The movement of Freud's work is toward interpreting the world as passion in his so-called "late" cultural texts, including "Beyond the Pleasure Principle". These texts supply the last word which unifies his theory.

There is no need for Freud to single out the concept of passion for discussion. His theory *is* a theory of passion. Freud's case studies are part of the movement of his work toward the cultural studies which interpret the world as passion, and his insistence, in the case of Dora, on locating her pathology in the vicissitudes of her sexual development, in apparent disregard of her family situation, is a link in that movement. It is not that Freud necessarily knew where he was going in that early case study, but rather that he ends it with a refusal of a last word, "I do not know what kind of help she wanted from me", which refuses the story of Dora's passion as the story of a struggle to leave behind that passion. If Freud had not yet formulated the theoretical point of his refusal at the time he published the case of Dora, he certainly felt the palpable presence of her resistance to giving up the transference as the problem that must be faced in interpreting it.

Freud's refusal of a last word has the effect on his theory of keeping open the question of what end passion pursues in repeating itself. If Dora is seeking to escape her passion, repeating it is a curious way to escape. It is easy to obscure the question Freud keeps open. Gallop, for instance, centers her discourse on the "keys to Dora", on "an insistent question" that Cixous and Clement "are asking" in their book, "La jeune née": "Is she a heroine or a victim?" The question pivots on the ambiguity of the hysteric: "she both contests and conserves. The hysteric contests inasmuch as she 'undoes family ties, introduces perturbation into the orderly unfolding of daily life, stirs up magic in apparent reason'. But the hysteric's contestation is contained and co-opted, and like any victory of the familiar, the familial over the heterogeneous and alien, this containment serves to strengthen the family."[29] Both the question and Gallop's discussion of it are appealing on a number of grounds, but both are possible only because they already presume that the story of Dora's passion is a story of a struggle to settle things with the forces that oppose the self's developmental movement toward its possibilities. Resistance, however, the repetition of the transference, opens up the question in Freud of what it is that passion wants by opening up the question of whether or not the developing self is under a compulsion to keep things unsettled, and where the only hope of keeping things unsettled is to repeat the family drama in different scenes and different settings as a passionate struggle that is like war.

After Dora come the Rat Man and the Wolf Man. Freud turns to the obsessive disorders in his clinical studies, where the transference is always an ambivalent love anxious to keep things unsettled, to explore the question of what it is that passion wants. The Rat Man and the Wolf Man are direct links to Freud's cultural texts in which he answers the question: Conflict is what passion wants. It is an answer which emerges from the light shed by the dark region in which instincts live, and where Freud has already indicated that psychoanalysis must find its home because it can only see from the illumination provided by darkness.

*

The obsessive is an uncanny figure for Freud, because he is disturbed precisely in those processes that underwrite the realization of possibilities in the social world. Unlike Hysteria, in which he saw disturbances arising from and affecting the erogenous areas, "obsessional neurosis stems from disturbances in the area... of 'dependent drives', that is, the drives to see, know, and possess..."[30] Like the hysteric, the obsessive lives narrative time as time's failure. Unlike the hysteric, the obsessive is a disturbance in that process of processes - thinking. Freud sees the memories of the obsessive returning as "thoughts", unlike hysterics for whom they return as "images".[31] It is thought that goes nowhere, consuming itself in what it cannot leave behind.

In the "Rat Man" case, the transference, no longer an obstacle to the process of cure, is recognized by Freud as the scene of treatment, the point of attack on the neurosis. For Freud, of course, this scene is a reenactment of the Oedipal scene - his great discovery which he invariably sees as the original moment at which desire encounters the authority of the world rendering the patient's future servile to his past. At the center of the scene of the transference is the analyst, always for Freud the substitute for the father made flesh from the reliquary of the past. The obsessive confers on the analyst, Bass points out, the power of "the one who knows"[32] - the possessor of the canons that render confusion coherent and to whom the obsessive must defer the truth of his own experience before he speaks. The obsessive's deference is riddled with conflict, revealing itself in the obsessive doubting which colors everything in his life. His pervasive doubting, Freud unequivocally tells us, "is in reality a doubt of his own love - which ought to be the most certain thing in his whole mind; and it becomes diffused over everything else, and is especially apt to become displaced on to what is most insignificant and small. A man who doubts his own love may, or rather must, doubt every lesser thing". [33]

Beneath the "Rat Man's" doubting of love, Freud tells us, are "thoughts about his father's death" which at an "early age had occupied his mind, and we may regard his illness itself as a reaction to that event, for which he had felt an obsessional wish fifteen years earlier. The strange extension of his obsessional fears to the 'next world' was nothing else than a compensation for these death-wishes which he had felt against his father".[34] What the "Rat Man" cannot leave behind are exaggerated narcissistic desires which leave their traces in "the omnipotence which he ascribed to his thought and feelings, and to his wishes, whether good or evil... This belief is a frank acknowledgement of a relic of the old megalomania of infancy..." [35]

In the "Rat Man" case Freud moves ambivalence - the psychological representation of instinctual conflict - to the center of the drama played out in the mind that is staged in the world. Freud's depiction of this drama in "meta-psychological" representations has not yet gone beyond the topographical divisions of the mind into Unconscious, Preconscious, and Conscious regions. He sums up the "Rat Man" case by stating: "I cannot take leave of my patient without putting on paper my impression that he had, as it were, disintegrated into three personalities, into one unconscious personality, that is to say, and into two preconscious ones between which his consciousness could oscillate".[36] The "oscillation" is between sadistic and masochistic strategies for fulfilling impossible narcissistic desires, which Freud speaks of as the signature of the obsessive. "The neurotic phenomena we have observed arise on the one hand from conscious feelings of affection which have become exaggerated as a reaction, and on the other hand from sadism persisting in the unconscious in the form of hatred".[37] Each scene of the "Rat Man's" transference fits Roustang's general formula for the drama the obsessive stages with his analyst: The scenes of transference love oscillate between masochistic strategies "of mastering the other by becoming the mirror image of the other in order to reverse the order of image and mirror", and sadistic strategies "of confusing the analyst by hiding behind the scene in order to create in the analyst the desire to see himself in the mirror of the obsessive by an act of submission". [38]

Freud identifies the elements in the "Rat Man's" transference but never organizes them into a coherent story about the desperate strategies of a subject desperate to realize himself as the subject of his own possibilities. Freud is not guided by the story of human development as the story of a fallen subject desperate for a recovery he could not achieve on his own. He never formulates a story of development structured by an end in which something is left behind. Freud may see, to use Mahony's terms, that "the Rat Man's optimal ego functioning was thwarted by a series of factors, among which numbered distorted self and object representations, massive reliance on obsessional defenses, taxing ego states that ranged from daze to listlessness to agitation, and the relentless self reproaches of a sadistic superego", but he does not tell the story of the "Rat Man's" suffering as one in which "in his disrupted narcissism, the Rat Man tried desperately to shore up his crumbling world."[39] Freud does not see that the "Rat Man's" suffering signifies "attempts at reparation and restitution [which] militated against healthy self esteem".[40] Nowhere does Freud's work contain an explicit vision of the end of development, even one as vaguely general as "healthy self esteem", from which a backward glance could render a patient's struggle with his history into a coherent story. Freud does not attempt a "reconstruction" of the "Rat Man's" "ego organization"[41] which would leave ambivalence behind. What we find in Freud, instead, is that ambivalence is never left behind.

The case of the Rat Man is a direct link to "Totem and Taboo". The dynamics of the obsessive are not the product of the failures of culture, about which revisionists can make as much or as little as they like. Culture, rather, is a metaphor for the dynamics disclosed in obsessive patients. Ambivalence is not the sign of a subject's struggle to leave behind a scene of narcissistic fantasies in order to enter a scene of possibilities; ambivalence is on the scene from the first as that which makes the scenes of the world possible.

In the beginning, Freud tells us, is ambivalence. Before culture there was a form of pre-social organization called the "primal horde". What "we find there is a violent and jealous father who keeps all the females for himself and drives away his sons as they grow up".[42] By Freud's own account this is not quite true. There is also the ambivalence of the sons toward the jealous father. We do not know how long this form of pre-social organization lasted, but "one day, the brothers who had been driven out came together, killed and devoured their father and so made an end of the patriarchal horde... The violent primal father had doubtless been the feared and envied model of each one of the company of brothers: and in the act of devouring him they accomplished their identification with him, and each one acquired a portion of his strength. The totem meal, which is perhaps mankind's earliest festival, would thus be a repetition and a commemoration of this memorable and criminal deed, which was the beginning of so many things - of social organization, of moral restrictions and of religion. In order that these latter consequences may seem plausible... we need only suppose that the tumultuous mob of brothers were filled with the same contradictory feelings which we can see at work in the ambivalent father complexes of our children and our neurotic patients. They hated their father, who presented such a formidable obstacle to their craving for power and their sexual desires; but they loved and admired him too. After they had got rid of him, had satisfied their hatred and had put into effect their wish to identify themselves with him, the affection which had all this time been pushed under was bound to make itself felt. It did so in the form of remorse. A sense of guilt made its appearance, which in this instance, coincided with the remorse felt by the whole group. The dead father became stronger than the living one had been - for events took the course we so often see them follow in human affairs to this day". [43]

The rebellion is not really a different scene interconnected to the next scene of its undoing. The rebellion and its undoing are a single scene comprising the beginning precisely because ambivalence is on the scene from the first as the curtain rises. Identification, for Freud, always presumes a prior ambivalence. But if the "primal horde" story presents ambivalence as the precondition for identification, it presents no precondition for ambivalence. Culture is not presented as the pole of attraction for a developmental movement that is the precondition for ambivalence. Ambivalence does not arise as the sign of a struggle to leave behind the narcissistic desires underlying the rebellion that would strangle the evolutionary movement toward culture. Just the reverse: the evolutionary movement toward culture, mediated by the identification with the father, arises as a consequence of ambivalence being first on the scene. The wish to identify with the dead father was a return to an original identification that coexisted from the first side by side with hate before the rebellion. The restoration of the murdered father by an oath to love him as if he still existed untouched by the movement of time was a return to the original scene of identification with the father with fear transposed to anxiety.

Freud's "primal horde" story appears at the end of "Totem and Taboo" which itself "is the end result of the analysis of obsessional neurotics".[44] Once Freud has told the story, it colors all of his cultural texts, moving like an arrow toward "Moses and Monotheism" which is "a completion and reinforcement" of "Totem and Taboo's" "repetitive and regressive theory".[45] Positioned at the end of "Totem and Taboo", the "primal horde" story stands as if it substitutes for the final word of a vision of cultural possibility that leaves ambivalence behind. Despite the glimpse Freud gives us of a transcendental story of cultural evolution following a scheme involving animistic, religious, and scientific phases,[46] "Totem and Taboo" describes the transference of the obsessional patient which leaves nothing behind, staged as human culture. It is a text that emphasizes the preservation of ambivalence beneath the surface of what ambivalence produces and reproduces as the scene of culture unfolding in historical time. The "primal horde" story at the end of "Totem and Taboo" can go nowhere because it is a beginning that repeats itself. It is a beginning that reduces the plot of history to the endlessly repeated variations of the single scene of a rebellion that, after crushing itself, continues to arise to crush itself.

This repetition is the true scandal of Freud's cultural texts. Kroeber and Malinowski[47] acknowledge and tame the scandal by refusing to take the "primal horde" story seriously as the story of the beginning of culture, while nevertheless conceding it to be of some value. It can be useful when read as allegorizing the development of conscience or the Superego during the socialization of a subject into culture. Read in these terms, the "primal horde" story releases culture from the sign of suspicion under which Freud puts it as a reproduction of the delirium of the obsessive. The concept "delirium", central to understanding the obsessive patient, is the invisible presence that organizes Freud's interpretation of culture. We find in the childhood history of the "Rat Man", Freud tells us, in addition to "an erotic instinct and a revolt against it... something more... namely a kind of delusion or delirium with the strange content that his parents knew his thoughts because he spoke them out loud without his hearing himself do it".[48] Culture is the father, and the father is the one who knows. Freud links the phenomenological precursor to what he later formulates in structural terms as "the Superego" with the concept of "delirium". Deliria are "hybrids between two species of thinking; they accept certain of the premises of the obsession they are combating, and thus, while using the weapons of reason, are established on the basis of pathological thought".[49] Reason, the language used by every culture in different idiomatic forms to guarantee the law as that which knows the right order of things, does not leave desire behind. The relationship between desire and reason is not one which holds between a parent and its child, but one which holds between a face and its mask. Culture cannot be made coherent by a story in which anything is left behind.

In both his case studies of obsessives as well as the cultural studies they anticipate, resistance and the transference are not identical. Freud does introduce possibility of thinking of resistance and transference as two sides of the same coin, in that there is the same reason for both, the defense against anxiety. But at the same time he "steadfastly refuses" to "lump" resistance with defense mechanisms.[50] What is decisive for Freud, Mannoni points out, is "the need to account for masochism, self reproaches, negative reactions, the universality of guilt feelings in general".[51] Of course, all of these are repeated in the transference which arises in relation to the analyst, but "when one steers a course between the two great principles of pleasure and reality... repetition... leaves a remnant... which seems impossible to justify"[52]. In Freud, the fact of resistance opens the question of "who resists?". This is the question that organizes Freud's case description of the "Wolf Man".

Despite a long analysis with Freud and a subsequent longer analysis with Ruth Mack Brunswick, the "Wolf Man's" treatment was a clear failure. The "Wolf Man" lived out his life in a series of remissions and exacerbations of his symptoms, relying toward the end, Mahony points out, "on medication as well as on a host of supportive psychiatrists and psychoanalysts" and finally leaving "this world in the wake of an analyst's illusion".[53] Mahony's judgment of Freud's case presentation is unequivocal, but not entirely uncomplimentary: "In his efforts to present the case of the Wolf Man as a referential rather than a persuasive treatise, Freud relies on some eye catching verbal acrobatics".[54] When "soberly looked at, the accumulative evidence suggests that the final course of treatment fulfilled Freud's own wishes and satisfied what had already been organized in his own mind; if some material was not forthcoming, other parts were tailored to fit expectations".[55] Freud's pyrotechnics resulted in a case study that is a fragmented residue of "partial truths"[56] waiting to be assembled into the narrative of a coherent psychoanalytic theory.

The problem is that Freud presents the story of the "Wolf Man's" development in the form of a circular movement. There is no end that can serve as a pole of attraction from which a coherent narrative can be structured. As his last word on the case Freud tells us that we are still left with the Wolf Man's "tenacity of fixation... his extraordinary propensity to ambivalence, and [as a third trait in a constitution which deserves the name of archaic] his power of maintaining simultaneously the most various and contradictory libidinal cathexes, all of them capable of functioning side by side. His constant wavering between these... was undoubtedly a trait belonging to the general character of the unconscious, which in his case had persisted into processes that had become conscious. But it showed itself only in the products of affective impulses; in the region of pure logic he betrayed, on the contrary, a peculiar skill in unearthing contradictions and inconsistencies." The delirium of the "Wolf Man" impresses Freud "in much the same way as the religion of Ancient Egypt, which is so unintelligible to us because it preserves the earlier stages of its development side by side with the end products..."[57] There is no confession in this case, as in the case of Dora, for example, that what is left over after the analysis is due to inadequately developed techniques for working with the transference. There is, rather, a theoretical coda which substitutes for an ending the notion of instinctual forces exerting a kind of magnetic power of attraction on the developmental movement to return to its original starting point: Instinct is "the nucleus of the unconscious, a primitive kind of mental activity, which would later be dethroned and overlaid by human reason, when that faculty came to be acquired, but which in some people, perhaps in every one, would retain the power of drawing down to it the higher mental processes".[58]

Freud superimposes on the circular movement of the "Wolf Man's" development a different figure of ambivalence than the oscillation between love and hate: the ambivalence between passivity and activity. This figure of ambivalence links the development of the "Wolf Man" to the configuration of the "Primal Horde" scene that ends "Totem and Taboo". The movement of the "Wolf Man's" development is from an original passivity to an activity that ends in a secondary passivity that repeats the original. The original passivity is a scene that must be reconstructed, like the "Primal Horde" scene, by the traces it leaves in the history of the "Wolf Man". The critical starting point for that reconstruction is the scene of the seduction of the "Wolf Man" at the age of three by his sister: "It was in spring, at a time when his father was away; the children were in one room playing on the floor, while their mother was working in the next. His sister had taken hold of his penis and played with it, at the same time telling him incomprehensible stories about his Nanya, as though by way of explanation".[59] It was a seduction in which the "Wolf Man" played a passive role which set into motion its ambivalent counterpart, sadistic activity, directed toward the sister and all the figures that came to substitute for her - Nanya his nurse, his subsequent governess, and all the small animals and insects he actually tormented as well as the "large animals [horses]..." he fantasized about tormenting.[60] He had, as well, "contemporary phantasies of quite another kind... boys beings chastised and beaten, and especially being beaten on the penis... His sadism had... turned round in phantasy against himself, and had been converted into masochism... This in accordance with the unusually clear, intense, and constant *ambivalence* of the patient, which was shown here for the first time in the even development of both members of the pairs of contrary component instincts".[61]

The trope that organizes the "Wolf Man's" movement through the chain of substitute figures, real and fantasized, that focus the play of his ambivalent feelings, is that of a restless search of sexual desire to master and dominate the source of its pleasure. It is a search that comes to rest its gaze on the father. "After his refusal by his Nanya his libidinal expectation detached itself from her and began to contemplate another person as a sexual object. This person was his father... He was no doubt led to this choice by a number of convergent factors... but above all he was in this way able to renew his first and most primitive object choice, which in conformity with a small child's narcissism, had taken place along the path of identification... It looks as though his seduction by his sister had forced him into a passive role, and had given him a passive sexual aim. Under the persistent influence of this experience he pursued a path from his sister via his Nanya to his father... His father was now his object once more..."[62] The sexual scene with the sister, in which he played a passive role, was like a way station on the road to a return to an original and more primitive passive relation to his father.

The play of the "Wolf Man's" ambivalence of passivity and activity is not a clinamen of the self's developmental axis grounded on one end in separation from the mother, and on the other end in the possibilities of the world. Freud's story of the "Wolf Man", rather, tracks the story of the "primal horde", beginning with the father and leading back to him. It leads back to the father with the additional element of anxiety over the threat of castration, which functions to preserve the father, precisely as it does in the "primal horde" scene: "The signs of an alteration in the patient's character were not accompanied by any symptoms of anxiety until after the occurrence of a particular event. Previously, it seems, there was no anxiety, while directly after the event the anxiety expressed itself in the most tormenting shape".[63] The "event" is the famous wolf dream "from which he awoke in a state of anxiety".[64] The restless search of the "Wolf Man's" sexual desire does not follow the pleasure principle. It is a search that follows a principle that is beyond the pleasure principle. The search ends with what it aimed at from the beginning: the "Wolf Man's" anxious and dreadful belief in a castrating father.

Freud clearly has a phallocentric view of the dynamics that govern the circular movement of development. But Freud's phallocentrism is not a celebration of the phallus. It is an interpretation of the law that governs the configuration of culture. For Freud, configuring culture is a male activity. While he leaves no doubt that he sees the male as the maker of history, it is trivial to think that he is arguing for a male world. Everybody loves some kind of law, because it is the bond to the law that makes a culture possible. But all lovers are anxious lovers because no one possesses a phallus but the law, and the law is always the Other which demands subservience from everyone, even the figures who claim to represent it, which is how we know it is the Law. This is why Freud puts history itself, made possible by the delirium of preserving through love what no one is or ever claims to be, under the sign of psychoanalytic suspicion, instructing us to interpret history to make sense of it. Establishing the frame of reference for interpreting history is what "Beyond the Pleasure Principle" is about, marking it as the foundation upon which Freud's cultural texts rest. We cannot expect too much substance from it beyond Freud's claim that only darkness illuminates the activity of life as a repetitive oscillation around an ambivalence that constitutes the limits of its possibilities.

"Beyond the Pleasure Principle" is Freud's most intense text. He has come far since the "Interpretation of Dreams", but only to find himself confronting the same image that haunted him at the beginning: "There is at least one spot in every dream at which it is unplumbable - a navel, as it were, that is its point of contact with the unknown".[65] He has reached the navel of the world knowing that he must venture into the darkness, leaving behind the disciplined deciphering of a language of desire that had hitherto been his guide. He knows he is foredoomed to produce a text that will be judged as even his admirers have come to judge it: as "profoundly baffling... only sporadically and superficially subordinated to logical imperatives..."[66] Although he declares he is writing it in order to see, he knows that there is nothing to see. It is a brave undertaking, because it invites precisely what it gets: the kind of elegiac praise that is designed to bury him.

As confused, murky and speculative as "Beyond the Pleasure Principle" is, it is nevertheless, a text whose point of departure is no less than the problem of interpreting the meaning of the world. The opening paragraph can be recast in the form of a question which governs the speculations that follow: If "in the theory of psycho-analysis we have no hesitation in assuming that the course taken by mental events is automatically regulated by the pleasure principle... that is to say, that the course of those events is invariably set into motion by an unpleasurable tension, and that it takes a direction such that its final outcome coincides with a lowering of that tension - that is, with an avoidance of unpleasure or a production of pleasure"[67] then why is the world not ruled by the pleasure principle? We are, in a sense, back to square one; back to the question Freud asked his first patients. This time Freud is not addressing the patient who invests his libido in the impossible rather than in the real, but the configuration of the world which is modeled by the passion of the patient's transference. In other words, he is asking, if passion seeks the world, what is it that passion wants? The question arises because "the details of the process by which repression turns a possibility of pleasure into a source of unpleasure are not yet clearly understood or cannot be clearly represented...", although psychoanalysis is not at a loss to explain why unpleasure appears as a "pleasure that cannot be felt as such".[68] The fact is that "most of the unpleasure that we experience is perceptual unpleasure: either perception of pressure by unsatisfied instincts, or external perception which is either distressing in itself or which excites unpleasurable expectations in the mental apparatus, that is, which is recognized by it as a 'danger'".[69] But after all is said and done, and we have subtracted the metapsychological explanations from the problem, we are still left with the notion of "danger" as a remainder. It is the same remainder as the fact of resistance - the patient's failure to take the last step toward his cure - on which every psychoanalytic discourse falters.

The fact of resistance leads Freud to examine anew "the mental reaction to external danger"[70] in the context of the traumatic neuroses for which "no complete explanation has yet been reached..."[71] In his discussion of the traumatic neuroses, Freud insists on the critical importance of maintaining a distinction between three mental reactions to external danger. Fright must be distinguished from anxiety, the reaction to an unknown danger, and from fear, the reaction to danger associated with a definite object. "Fright... is the name we give to the state a person gets into when he has run into danger without being prepared for it; it emphasizes the factor of surprise".[72] With respect to the traumatic neuroses, "the chief weight in their causation seems to rest upon the factor of surprise, of fright".[73]

The notion of a danger that surprises is the most ancient and enduring trope for the figure of death. It is the compulsion to repeat that leads us to the danger that surprises which lies at the origin of the principle beyond the pleasure principle. Freud sees this compulsion in his little nephew's famous "fort-da" game played by "taking any small objects he could get hold of and throwing them away from him into a corner, under the bed, and so on, so that hunting for his toys and picking them up was quite a business".[74] This leads Freud to take us, once again, through the subtraction of psychoanalytic explanations of development to a remainder left over. This time he leads us to the remainder through a consideration of the transference as the patient's struggle with his history. It is indisputably true, says Freud, that "the early efflorescence of infantile sexual life is doomed to come to an end because its wishes are incompatible with reality and with the inadequate stage of development which the child has reached". It is also indisputably true that "that efflorescence perishes in the most distressing circumstances and to the accompaniment of the most painful feelings. Loss of love and failure leave behind them a permanent injury to self- assurance in the form of a narcissistic scar..." Finally, it is indisputably true that although attempts to recover this lost narcissism are doomed to failure, "patients repeat all of these unwanted situations and painful emotions in the transference and revive them with the greatest ingenuity".[75] It is one thing to attribute this "to *active* behavior on the part of the person concerned... when we can discern in him an essential character-trait which always remains the same and which is compelled to find expression in a repetition of the same experiences." But "we are much more impressed by cases where the subject appears to have a *passive* experience, over which he has no influence, but in which he meets with a repetition of the same fatality".[76] Freud cites as exemplary "the... moving poetic picture of a fate... given by Tasso in his romantic epic Gerulsalemme Liberata. Its hero, Tancred, unwittingly kills his beloved Clorinda in a duel while she is disguised in the armor of an enemy knight. After her burial he makes his way into a strange magic forest which strikes the Crusaders' army with terror. He slashes with his sword at a tall tree; but blood streams from the cut and the voice of Clorinda, whose soul is imprisoned in the tree, is heard complaining that he has wounded his beloved once again".[77]

The difference does not make a difference. Freud has displaced us from the region ruled over by mistake, accident or error. He is moving us into that region where "we shall find courage to assume that there really does exist in the mind a compulsion to repeat which overrides the pleasure principle".[78] The darkness has assumed a palpable presence with the presence of the patient's resistance in the psychoanalytic discourse: "The phenomena of transference are obviously exploited by the resistance the ego maintains in its pertinacious insistence upon repression; the compulsion to repeat, which the treatment tries to bring into its service, is as it were, drawn over to its side, (clinging as the ego does to the pleasure principle)".[79]

It is time to explore the darkness that illuminates the world as the compulsion to repeat the transference. It is clear that "the quantity of excitation that is present in the mind but is not in any way 'bound'"[80] is the source of the fright that surprises. Freud's concept of "unbound excitations" is not a euphemism for "chaos" against which humans struggle to give their world a meaning represented by the cultures they invent. Narcissistic fantasies are not misplaced efforts of human subjects to make meaning out of chaos. The notion of "unbound excitations" opens up the problem of the intentional structures that occupy the darkness which pose the threat of a danger that surprises.

The compulsion to repeat does not point to chaos opposed to structure, but to structure opposed to structure.

Freud knows where he is going, leading us there through a master metaphor that tropes the idea of a danger that surprises. In the beginning "there is this little fragment of living substance... suspended in the middle of an external world charged with the most powerful energies; and it would be killed by the stimulation emanating from these if it were not provided with a protective shield against stimuli".[81] A "just so" story that shadows the primal horde story, also a fable about a primordial passivity at the origin of life that is compulsively repeated. The development of a protective shield is like the rebellion of the sons - a reversal of passivity to activity upon which the survival of life itself depends. With the idea of a protective shield, Freud boldly asserts, we are in a position to more fully understand "the Kantian theorem that time and space are 'necessary forms of thought'".[82] What it comes down to in the end is that the shield evolves into the "system Pcpt.-Cs".[83] The ratio of strong stimuli outside to weaker inside has been reversed, and life is activated, with the "system Pcpt.- Cs" in place to perform its most essential function as a shield - the monitoring of danger from the outside. But first the internal danger which the reversal of the ratio of strong to weak stimuli has created to allow life to move forward into the space of the world must be made into an external danger.

The human world of meaning is ready to be born. "Toward the inside there can be no... shield; the excitations in the deeper layers extend into the system directly and in undiminished amount, insofar as certain of their characteristics give rise to feelings in the pleasure-unpleasure series".[84] The way life deals with these dangerous excitations on the inside that can surprise us, in order to protect itself as life, is "to treat them as though they were acting, not from the inside, but from the outside, so that it may be possible to bring the shield against stimuli into operation as a means of defense against them. This is the origin of *projection*, which is destined to play such a large part in the causation of pathological processes".[85] The last sentence invites us to interpret the human world, arising from projection, as a symptom.

We have gone beyond the pleasure principle, and are ready to return to it through the one mental event with which psychoanalysis will always be identified: the dream. "The function of dreams, which consists in setting aside any motives that might interrupt sleep, by fulfilling the wishes of the disturbing impulses, is not the original function. It would not be possible for them to perform that function until the whole mental life had accepted the dominance of the pleasure principle".[86] The original function of dreams takes place "at a time before the purpose of dreams was the fulfillment of wishes".[87] This function is pointed to by the traumatic dreams of those suffering from traumatic neuroses: "It is not in the service of [the pleasure] principle that the dreams of patients suffering from traumatic neuroses lead them back with such regularity to the situation in which the trauma occurred. We may assume rather, that dreams are here helping to carry out another task, which must be accomplished before the dominance of the pleasure principle can even begin. These dreams are endeavoring to master the stimulus retrospectively, by developing the anxiety whose omission was the cause of the traumatic neurosis". [88]

Once we follow Freud beyond the pleasure principle, we follow him beyond the original idea that virtually gave birth to psychoanalysis - namely, that the fulfillment of the pleasure principle is doomed to founder on anxiety. We follow him instead into the darker and more perplexing idea which governed his analysis of the "Wolf Man" case: the pleasure principle arises from the *discovery* of anxiety in order to *preserve* anxiety in the form of the dread of castration located in the figure of the father. It is a story of the world as the repetition of the transference that Freud is telling. Without anxiety life cannot be preserved, and the preservation of anxiety as castration anxiety preserves and multiplies the father as the axis along which the repetitious scenes of history unfold. History is the repetition of a single scene of a rebellion against the figure of the tyrannical father that crushes itself by preserving the father that crushes the rebellion.

The philosopher, Bernard-Henri Levy, inspired in part by Freud, is right to re-think our most treasured ideas about power. "Freud suggests at least one thing. Perhaps 'power' means nothing but the 'will to live' or the 'will to survive'".[89] The social bond is not the antidote to power. The social bond is power. "Power has always been defined as a principle springing from a source and flowing into its branches. It must be defined in the opposite way, as an effect that comes from below, returns from the periphery, and rises from the depths of the world. It has always been described as though it were a plague, a strange disease attacking a healthy body, spreading terror and corrupting innocence. We have to reverse the metaphor and describe it as a returning tide, the smell of a diseased body which has been corrupted from the very beginning and terrorized from within. It has always been said that the ruled internalize violence, identify with the Prince, and swallow his orders. Why not, on the contrary, imagine a hemorrhage, an expulsion of the Prince, and an externalization of the law?"[90]

The metaphors of power could be Freud's. But Levy does not think power through as far as Freud does. To think power through to its limits means going beyond power. What is preserved in order to preserve the world is not power, but conflict. There is power, and there is the Prince, and there are the Prince's subjects who feel the pressure of his violence, yet no one owns power. Power is absent everywhere which is why there is only the conflict over it. Power is only a pretext for conflict. The conflict that goes on between the patient and the analyst is the transference that models the world. The countertransference, never absent in the analyst, is not an error, a mistake, or a deficiency in technique. The transference belongs to the entire analytic scene, not just to the patient. It is the entire scene of the transference that is staged in the world as the oscillating sado-masochistic conflict that goes on between the patient and analyst. How could Freud not know it? This conflict was the scene of his life spent with the very followers he called on to help him formulate a psychoanalytic theory.

The world arises as conflict and is preserved through the preservation of conflict. We have finally reached, in "Beyond the Pleasure Principle", the great drama that goes on in the darkness, leaving its traces in the content of mental life. "How is the predicate of being 'instinctual' related to the compulsion to repeat?"[91] The answer rests on the most fundamental reversal of all: "We may have come upon the track of a universal attribute of the instincts and perhaps of organic life in general which has not hitherto been clearly recognized or at least not explicitly stressed. It seems, then, that an instinct is a compulsion inherent in organic life to restore an earlier state of things which the living entity has been obliged to abandon under the pressure of external disturbing forces; that is, it is a kind of organic elasticity, or, to put it another way, the expression of the inertia inherent in organic life".[92] Freud does not ground these remarks in psychoanalytic interpretations of the symbols produced by mind. We are dealing with processes that have no counterparts in any psychic purposes, wishes or desires. This is what makes "Beyond the Pleasure Principle" such an uncomfortably speculative text in which Freud appears to wander around in the dark. He will not abandon psychoanalytic interpretation that starts from the mystery of human desire or the teleological frame of reference which must govern psychoanalytic interpretation. Yet he is compelled to separate psychoanalytic interpretation from a language of desire which supports it in order to illuminate by darkness the ends desire pursues.

Freud turns to the spawning behavior of fish and the migratory flights of birds in order to conclude that behind "the deceptive appearance of... forces tending towards change and progress" is the pursuit of an "ancient goal by paths alike old and new".[93] Death is not an event that interferes with life, it is the goal of life. "If we are to take it as a truth that knows no exception that everything living dies for internal reasons - becomes inorganic once again - then we shall be compelled to say that 'the goal of all life is death' and, looking backwards, that 'what was inanimate existed before what is living'".[94] Freud throws into question all of the panoply of instincts that he had once formulated to valorize human effort. "The hypothesis of self-preservative instincts, such as we attribute to all living beings, stands in marked opposition to the idea that instinctual life as a whole serves to bring about death. Seen in this light, the theoretical importance of the instincts of self-preservation, of self-assertion and of mastery greatly diminishes. They are component instincts whose function it is to assure that the organism shall follow its own path to death, and to ward off any possible ways of returning to inorganic existence other than those which are imminent in the organism itself".[95] The image evoked is precisely that of birds and fish struggling to reach their breeding and spawning grounds. Freud, whose theory complicated our view of human psychology almost beyond measure is determined to build a case about that complexity using the most tenuous of arguments by analogy. "What we are left with is the fact that the organism wishes to die only in its own fashion." Instincts, "these guardians of life... were originally the myrmidons of death. Hence arises the paradoxical situation that the living organism struggles most energetically against events [dangers, in fact] which might help it to attain its life's goal rapidly, by a kind of short circuit".[96] With the idea of a "struggle against short circuiting", Freud is no longer speaking like a naturalist drawing simple analogies. This is the Freud who knows that we can grasp the complicated content of the mental representations of human desire only through the richest and darkest dramaturgical metaphors describing a drama without psychological representations that takes place in the very cells of the body. The complex bodies of higher organisms have evolved so that "the germ cells... with their full complement of inherited and freshly acquired instinctual dispositions, separate themselves from the organism as a whole... These germ cells, therefore, work against the death of the living substance and succeed in winning for it what we can only regard as potential immortality, though that may mean no more than a lengthening of the road to death... The instincts which watch over the destinies of these elementary organisms that survive the whole individual... constitute the group of the sexual instincts... They are the true life instincts. They operate against the purpose of the other instincts, which leads by reasons of their function, to death; and this fact indicates that there is an opposition between them and the other instincts, an opposition whose importance was long ago recognized by the theory of the neuroses".[97]

We are returning to the complexities of human desire revealed in that single primordial scene of the primal horde; the scene of a rebellion crushing itself. Culture arises out of this scene as a break with the natural rhythm of instinctual life. "It is as though the life of the organism moved with a vacillating rhythm. One group of instincts rushes forward so as to reach the final goal of life as swiftly as possible; but when a particular stage in the advance has been reached, the other group jerks back to a certain point to make a fresh start and so prolong the journey".[98] Culture is generated by the conflict between "the ego or death instincts and the sexual or life instincts",[99] both of which seek to lead the organism to death, one directly without hesitation and the other by prolonging life to protect the germ cells. "The repressed instinct never ceases to strive for complete satisfaction which would consist in the repetition of a primary experience of satisfaction. No substitutive or reactive formations and no sublimations will suffice to remove the repressed instinct's persisting tension... ; The backward path that leads to complete satisfaction is as a rule obstructed by the resistances that maintain the repressions. So there is no alternative but to advance in the direction in which growth is still free - though with no prospect of bringing the process to a conclusion or of being able to reach the goal".[100] History is a story without a last word, repeating the same theme in each of its different scenes. The scenes of the transference repeat the scene of the primal horde; and the scenes of the transference model the history of culture.

Even though Freud claimed he could not do without the ideas in "Beyond the Pleasure Principle" his revisionists usually express puzzlement over why he wrote a text that is a melange of energistic and biological analogies embroidered around a bizarre notion of a death instinct. Yet the structure of the story that "Beyond the Pleasure Principle" tells is not as bizarre and disorganized as it seems. In the first place, it is relevant to the problem that it addresses - understanding why resistance is at the center of the transference carried into the world as the world. In the second place, if we bracket Freud's mixed language of an instinctual energetics that causes meaning to represent its intentions, then the story he is telling in "Beyond the Pleasure Principle" is a story of culture recognizable as a cautionary tale about what it is that passion wants. In a sense, Freud is doing no more with respect to the world than de Rougemont does in his classic studies of the romantic myths of passion, whose archetype is the Romance of Tristan and Iseult: disclosing passion's "bold and simple design, a kind of archetype of our most complex feelings of unrest".[101] Passion is always a story about lovers struggling against the obstacles that keep them apart. But the story of their struggle is the story of their ambivalence - of wanting distance from each other, of the cunning repetition of a struggle which resists going somewhere, resists settling things, resists an end. In Tristan, "everything the knight and princess do betrays that they act in virtue of a necessity they are unaware of - and that perhaps the author has been unaware of too - but that is stronger than the need of their happiness. Objectively, not one of the barriers to the fulfillment of their love is insuperable, and yet each time they give up. It is not too much to say that they never miss a chance of getting parted. When there is no obstruction, they invent one, as in the case of the drawn sword and Tristan's marriage. They invent obstructions as if on purpose, notwithstanding that such barriers are their bane."[102] Passion is always a story which invents its history by establishing a distance that unsettles things through relating the sublime, which commands the subordination of love, to a violence that fills that distance. In Freud's terms, passion depends for its history on establishing the paternal bond.

And beneath the story whose history depends on repeating a struggle that invents distance, passion is always a love story about wanting death. "A myth is needed to express the dark and unmentionable fact that passion is linked with death, and involves the destruction of anyone yielding himself up to it with all his strength."[103] Passion must always be read as a cautionary tale which puts love under the sign of suspicion for masking as death. If this is the lens through which we must read tales of passion, then "Beyond the Pleasure Principle" is a disclosure of the world as a cautionary tale of passion whose foundation is the transference. It's a text which functions in Freud's theory to outline its end, the last word toward which it aims, which is later filled in by the density of his cultural texts. What gives narrative closure to the totality of Freud's work is a warning about the dangers of love masking as the love of death first sounded in "Beyond the Pleasure Principle". It is the power of love that carries the danger and the warning. It carries them not because its power is a primordial one capable of being shaped by the scenes of the world, but because its power shapes the scenes of the world into passions which cannot stop courting a danger which we will never understand except in terms of other powers acting in the darkness offstage. This is implied by the question de Rougemont insists we must confront when we confront the power of the myths of passion to repeat themselves. We know the historical dates at which the myths of "Tristan, Faust, Hamlet, and Don Juan" emerged "into the world literature... and developed all their contagious and revealing powers." They "are indeed the imaginative creations of a Beroul, a Marlowe, a Shakespeare, and a Tirso de Molina... But another question immediately arises: have these authors invented or discovered their characters?"[104] In more general terms, "where do the myths come from? Are they our inventions, or are we theirs?"[105] It is a question that would be immediatly recognizable to Freud. "Beyond the Pleasure Principle" is a mythologizing of the instincts in order to illuminate the meaning of the myths of love that shape the world in the form of the paternal bond whose repetition he called the transference. As long as there is a world we cannot stop living it as figures of passion. But Freud's theory moves in a direction toward a warning about love which defines the work of consciousness that justifies psychoanalysis as a work of placing love under suspicion.

Such a movement appears to be out of the question when the self as agent is the center of the story of its development. The self is centered by being defined in terms of what governs its development: a need for objects which organize the direction of its agency. In another words, centering the self as agency in the story of its own development, privileges the concept of "need" in defining the experiences which govern its development; and "need" is an absence defined by the object it aims at. Every reading of Freud, from the scene of completing him, is a dream to author psychoanalytic theory as a love story about choosing visions of possibility over impossibility by choosing right objects to love. Visions of possibility aim at a language of psychoanalysis that will address us in the ancient language of culture - the language of a didactics about loving. As such, Freud's theory cannot avoid being a subversive polemic that haunts the revisionist scene of reading him like a scandal.

No revisionist of Freud's work shows us this more clearly than Jean-Paul Sartre. It is not strange to identify Sartre as a psychoanalytic revisionist. His famous refusal of the unconscious is neither a refusal of the unconscious nor a refusal of psychoanalysis. It is a preface, rather, to his announcement that his program for revising psychoanalytic theory, including revising the meaning of the concept "unconscious" which is as central to his proposed psychoanalysis as it is to Freud's, "has not yet found its Freud". He leaves no doubt as to who that will be by following immediately with the statement that "at most we can find the foreshadowing of it in certain particularly successful biographies."[106] We should not be surprised at Sartre's ambition to substitute himself for Freud, an ambition that it is not unreasonable to say governed much of the evolution of his work. There is a close kinship between them. What Lionel Trilling says of Freud could just as easily be said of Sartre: "Freud's positiveness, his belief that truth could actually be found, is also the sign of something particular in his temperament, particular in his vision of the world. It is an aspect of his response to the pain of life, the mark of his moral urgency, of his deep therapeutic commitment to the human cause".[107] Reciprocally, what Iris Murdoch says of Sartre could just as easily be said of Freud: "A driving force in all his writing is his serious desire to change the life of his reader... [He is] concerned to persuade and communicate."[108] Sartre's biographies, which he foresaw as the successful vehicles for conveying his version of psychoanalysis, are almost universally regarded as peculiar pieces of work, more fiction than biography. They are neither, but as we shall elaborate later, follow the logic of psychoanalytic case studies which Freud himself feared would be read as fiction.

The movement in Sartre's work through his three main "biographical" studies, Baudelaire, Genet and Flaubert, is a movement into the revisionist scene of reading Freud which lays bare the most fundamental structures which Freud's work subverts. In the beginning, in "Being and Nothingness", and in its predecessor, "Nausea", Sartre assumed the role of shattering the coherency of human lives. Yet the power of love as a vision of human possibility that unifies them is already present. In other words, in the beginning, when Sartre puts the meaning of everything into motion, unsettling the meaning of everything, he is already a passion to leave nothing unsettled, to write psychoanalysis as a love story that settles the meaning of everything. The way Sartre saw his relationship to Freud throughout his work is indicated by a screen play he wrote about Freud's early psychoanalytic discoveries commissioned by John Huston but never used because it would have made a seven hour movie.[109] There is, as Pontalis has commented, nothing novel in it.[110] We can read into its banality Sartre's vision of Freud, the great inventor of psychoanalysis who was unable to stand anywhere but at the center of traditional nineteenth century science. Freud's work is supported by archaic established beliefs. It is Sartre who stands on the margins, on the cutting edge where psychoanalysis can fulfill its original promise to change established beliefs which imprison the self. In its way, Sartre's screen play, his case study of Freud, is standard revisionist fare. But was Sartre ever on the margins? Was Freud ever in the center? Sartre's revision of psychoanalytic theory into a didactics of love helps put into relief the full weight of Freud's warning about love in his cultural texts which haunts all revisionists, turning their last words against them.

References

1. Patrick J. Mahony, *Freud and the Rat Man*, New Haven, Yale University Press, 1986, p. 91.

2. J. Laplanche and J.-B. Pontalis, *The Language of Psychoanalysis*, tr. Donald Nicholson-Smith, New York, W. W. Norton, 1973, p. 457.

3. Sigmund Freud, "Fragment of an Analysis of a Case of Hysteria", *Standard Edition* 7: p. 119.

4. Steven Marcus, "Freud and Dora: Story, History, Case History", in Edith Kurzweil and William Phillips, eds. *Literature and Psychoanalysis*, New York, Columbia University Press, 1983, p. 159.

5. Ibid., p. 159.

6. Ibid., p. 160.

7. Ibid., p. 165.

8. Sigmund Freud, SE 7, p. 28.

9. Ibid., p. 28.

10. Ibid., p. 28.

11. Ibid., p. 28.

12. Ibid., p. 28.

13. Ibid., p. 31.

14. Ibid., p. 31.

15. Quoted in Steven Marcus, p. 162.

16. Sigmund Freud, SE 7, p. 32.

17. Ibid., p. 119.

18. Ibid., p. 120.

19. Ibid., p. 122

20. Ibid., p. 118.

21. Erik H. Erikson, *Insight and Responsibility*, New York, W. W. Norton, 1964, p. 161.

22. Ibid., p. 169.

23. Ibid., p. 169-170.

24. Ibid., p. 169.

25. Ibid., p. 170.

26. Jules Glenn, "Freud's Adolescent Patients: Katharina, Dora and the 'Homosexual Woman'" in Mark Kanzer and Jules Glenn eds., *Freud and His Patients*, New York, Jason Aronson, 1980, p. 29.

27. Therese Benedek, "Ambivalence, Passion, and Love", *Journal of the American Psychoanalytic Association*, 25:1, 1977, p. 53.

28. Bruno Bettelheim, *Freud and Man's Soul*, New York, Alfred A. Knopf, 1983, p. 109.

29. Jane Gallop, *The Daughter's Seduction: Feminism and Psychoanalysis*, Ithaca, N.Y., Cornell University Press, 1982, p. 133.

30. Mahony, 1986, p. 160.

31. Ibid., p. 152.

32. Alan Bass, "The Double Game: An Introduction", in Joseph H. Smith and William Kerrigan eds., *Taking Chances: Derrida, Psychoanalysis, and Literature*, Baltimore, The Johns Hopkins University Press, 1984, p. 81.

33. Sigmund Freud, "Notes Upon a Case of Obsessional Neurosis", *Standard Edition*, V. 10, p. 241.

34. Ibid., p. 235.

35. Ibid., p. 233-234.

36. Ibid., p. 248.

37. Ibid., p. 240.

38. Francois Roustang, *Dire Mastery*, tr. Ned Lukacher, Baltimore, The Johns Hopkins University Press, 1982, p. 56.

39. Mahony, 1986, p. 66.

40. Ibid., p. 66-67.

41. Judith S. Kestenberg, "Ego-Organization in Obsessive-Compulsive Development. A Study of the Rat Man, Based on Interpretation of Movement Patterns", in Kanzer and Glenn, 1980, p. 144.

42. Sigmund Freud, "Totem and Taboo", *Standard Edition*, V. 13, p. 141.

43. Ibid., p. 141-143.

44. O. Mannoni, *Freud*, tr. Renaud Bruce, New York, Pantheon, 1971, p. 132.

45. Paul Ricoeur, *Freud and Philosophy*, tr. Denis Savage, New Haven, Yale University Press, 1970, p. 244.

46. Sigmund Freud, SE, 13, p. 90.

47. Leszek Kolakowski, "The Psychoanalytic Theory of Culture" in Robert Boyers, ed., *Psychological Man*, New York, Harper Colophon, 1975, p. 43-44.

48. Sigmund Freud, SE, 10, p. 163-164.

49. Ibid., p. 222.

50. Laplanche and Pontalis, 1973, p. 395.

51. Mannoni, 1971, p. 145.

52. Ibid., p. 148.

53. Patrick J. Mahony, *Cries of the Wolf Man*, New York, International Universities Press, 1984, p. 7-8.

54. Ibid., p. 100.

55. Ibid., p. 102.

56. Ibid., p. 103.

57. Sigmund Freud, "From the History of an Infantile Neurosis", *Standard Edition*, V. 17, p. 119.

58. Ibid., p. 120.

59. Ibid., p. 20.

60. Ibid., p. 26.

61. Ibid., p. 26.

62. Ibid., p. 27.

63. Ibid., p. 28.

64. Ibid., p. 28.

65. Sigmund Freud, *The Interpretation of Dreams*, tr. James Strachey, New York, Basic Books, 1955, p. 111.

66. Jean Laplanche, *Life and Death in Psychoanalysis*, tr. Jeffrey Mehlman, Baltimore, The Johns Hopkins University Press, 1976, p. 107.

67. Sigmund Freud, "Beyond the Pleasure Principle", *Standard Edition*, V. 18, p. 7.

68. Ibid., p. 11.

69. Ibid., p. 11.

70. Ibid., p. 11.

71. Ibid., p. 12.

72. Ibid., p. 12.

73. Ibid., p. 12.

74. Ibid., p. 14.

75. Ibid., p. 21.

76. Ibid., p. 22.

77. Ibid., p. 22.

78. Ibid., p. 22.

79. Ibid., p. 23.

80. Ibid., p. 26.

81. Ibid., p. 27.

82. Ibid., p. 28.

83. Ibid., p. 28.

84. Ibid., p. 29.

85. Ibid., p. 29.

86. Ibid., p. 32.

87. Ibid., p. 32.

88. Ibid., p. 32.

89. Bernard-Henri Levy, *Barbarism With a Human Face*, tr. George Holoch, New York, Harper Colophon Books, 1979, p. 18.

90. Ibid., p. 13.

91. Sigmund Freud, SE, 18, p. 36.

92. Ibid., p. 36.

93. Ibid., p. 38.

94. Ibid., p. 38.

95. Ibid., p. 39.

96. Ibid., p. 39.

97. Ibid., p. 40.

98. Ibid., p. 41.

99. Ibid., p. 44.

100. Ibid., p. 42.

101. Denis de Rougemont, *Love in the Western World*, tr. Montgomery Belgion, Garden City, Doubleday Anchor, 1957, p. 4.

102. Ibid., p. 26.

103. Ibid., p. 8.

104. Denis de Rougemont, *Love Declared*, tr. Richard Howard, New York, Pantheon, 1963, p. 16.

105. Ibid., p. 15.

106. Jean-Paul Sartre, *Existential Psychoanalysis*, tr. Hazel E. Barnes, Chicago, Henry Regnery (Gateway Edition), p. 59.

107. Lionel Trilling, *Gathering of Fugitives*, Boston, Beacon Press, 1956, p. 57.

108. Iris Murdoch, *Sartre: Romantic Rationalist*, New Haven, Yale University Press, 1953, p. ix.

109. Jean-Paul Sartre, *The Freud Scenario*, tr. Quintin Hoare, Chicago, The University of Chicago Press, 1985, p. viii.

110. Ibid., p. xv.

Part 3

Sartre's Passion

From the beginning of his own work Sartre unequivocally fixes the role he is to play throughout his scene of reading Freud. "For Freud" writes Sartre in "Being and Nothingness", "as for us an act can not be limited to itself; it refers immediately to more profound structures".[1] To understand an act is to interpret it in terms of the meaning it has for a desiring subject who inserts meaning into the world in pursuit of the satisfaction of his desires. An act always has a particular meaning for a subject which must be understood as a part that represents the whole. "The problem... is to disengage the meanings implied by an act - by every act - and to proceed from there to richer and more profound meanings until we encounter the meaning which does not imply any other meaning and which refers only to itself".[2] By the end of his work, neither Sartre's notion that such an original meaning "refers only to itself", nor his fiat that the search for the meaning of a subject's acts begins and ends with the history of the subject, is viable. What never loses viability for Sartre is that properly revised, psychoanalysis is the indispensable "method which enables us to make these structures explicit".[3]

What commends Freud to Sartre in "Being and Nothingness" is that "the act appears to Freud *symbolic*; that is, it seems to him to express a more profound desire..."[4] An act, in effect, is a gesture desire makes toward the world in an effort to satisfy itself. Freud's theory, however, fails the principles of its method. Desire, in Freud, "could be interpreted only in terms of an initial determination of the subject's libido". Sartre's damning judgment is that "affectivity for Freud is at the basis of the act in the form of psycho - physiological drives".[5] True "this affectivity is originally in each of us a *tabula rasa*...", but all this means is that "for Freud the external circumstances, and so to speak, the *history* of the subject will decide whether this or that drive will be fixed on this or that object".[6] Freud who developed a method for understanding the actions of a subject in precisely the concrete terms that Sartre insists a subject's acts must be understood - in terms of intentionally purposive humans who insert human reality into the world in pursuit of their desires - then developed a theory which subverts his own method. Freud's theory transposes the acts of a concrete thinking, feeling and desiring human subject into the acts of a piece of nature indistinguishable from any other causally determined object. "Consequently the dimension of the future does not exist for psychoanalysis. Human reality... must be interpreted solely by a regression toward the past from the standpoint of the present".[7]

Sartre saw himself facing a psychoanalytic theory for which the subject had never been the subject. In Freud "the fundamental structures of the subject, which are signified by its acts, are not so signified *for him* but for an objective witness who uses discursive methods to make these meanings explicit...And this is just since in spite of everything his acts are only a result of the past, which is on principle out of reach, instead of seeking to inscribe their goal on the future".[8] Sartre is all but saying that to found a method of understanding on a principle that puts the future out of reach of the desiring subject, is to found a method on a symptom not a theory. It is Sartre who will hold psychoanalysis fast to its promise to define a liberating work of consciousness.

In Sartre's work, from beginning to end, freedom defines the human subject whose road to freedom is a psychoanalytic work of consciousness that leaves behind the paternal bond. The history of Sartre's work unfolds as a passion to formulate a vision of possibility which, by defining freedom guides a subject's work toward realizing what he is. Freud haunts this history as if he were an invisible interlocutor questioning the meaning of Sartre's passion to complete him. Sartre never sees Freud playing the role of his interlocutor. LaCapra puts it accurately enough: Sartre's "readings tend to be selective, one-way appropriations that do not recognize the other as having a voice, especially in respects that might generate radical doubts about his own framework of interpretation".[9] This is no doubt related to the fact that Sartre never thought of himself as part of an evolving history of a psychoanalytic revisionist discourse. Sartre never shows any interest in the history of psychoanalytic theory. Throughout his work he sustains the tone he set in "Being and Nothingness", conflating Freud with his revisionists to oppose himself to a timeless entity called "psychoanalysis", a name he freely interchanges with the name "Freud". Nevertheless the entire movement of Sartre's work toward its end is a radical reconstruction of Freud's theory marked at every step by the problem of defining consciousness as a work whose object is to liberate the subject from being lost to himself in his own false consciousness. In "Being and Nothingness", by calling for the subject to become the subject of psychoanalysis, Sartre is already part of the revisionist discourse that seeks to complete psychoanalysis. By the end of his work Sartre is not only firmly part of the revisionist scene of reading Freud, but his work is virtually paradigmatic of the narrative which emerges from that scene.

Sartre's passionate pursuit to complete psychoanalysis can be traced through his three major biographies of Baudelaire, Genet and Flaubert. This trio of works which bear the names of real people pose a problem: How shall we read them since they seem to violate the standards and purposes that define the genre of biography? Do they really belong to it? Sartre seems uninterested in presenting anything remotely like an objective view of their lives. He is highly selective in what he presents as significant events in their chronology. For example, all three were writers, and "all three", LaCapra points out, actually "were brought to trial - Baudelaire and Flaubert for what they wrote, and Genet for the criminal acts later celebrated in his works. Sartre does not take the way his subjects were treated in courts of law as an object for extended study".[10] He is, in general, as Collins observes, "faithless to the calendar time of his subjects", focusing rather on what he regards as "the more essential internal experience of time..."[11] We are forced to be suspicious of this selective interest in their lives. Sartre, in describing what he takes to be the critical event in Genet's childhood, tells us "that was how it happened, in that or some other way".[12] In his study of Flaubert, after a lengthy theoretical discourse on the significance of how his mother's care shaped Flaubert's life, Sartre casually remarks, "This is a fabrication, I confess. I have no proof that it was so."[13] If these are biographies we have a right to expect more. These are, after all, real people Sartre is studying, and we have the right to know the truth about their lives, or at least as much of the truth that a biographer can unearth. Sartre seems to confuse fiction with biography, writing works that occupy an interstitial space between a concern for and indifference to biographical truth. As Scriven states about "The Family Idiot", it seems to be "a book about nothing, an imaginary book about the imaginary existence of a nineteenth century French novelist, a colossal literary folly symbolizing the disjunction between the aspirations of the writer and the requirements of the reading public... Sartre makes no real attempt to address himself to the concerns of his readership. The primary preoccupations in the 'Flaubert' are Sartre's own. He freely researches whatever avenue of research he pleases, with the result that however rewarding the experience may have been for Sartre the reader is left frustrated, dissatisfied".[14] Although the tone may vary, one would have to look far to find a radically different judgment applied to each of Sartre's biographies.

It is possible, however, not only to make sense of his studies of Baudelaire, Genet and Flaubert, but also discover the uniquely peculiar logic they follow for analyzing a life history, if we read them as the equivalent of psychoanalytic case studies. His subjects are like phantom patients whose lives he attempts to disclose following the logic imposed on every psychoanalyst. Sartre as much as tells us this, particularly with reference to the "Flaubert" that is his capstone work which he discusses more often than the others. In the preface to "The Family Idiot" he tells us that one of the reasons he chose to write about Flaubert is that "Flaubert's early works and his correspondence... appear... to consist of the strangest, the most easily deciphered revelations. We might imagine we were hearing a neurotic 'free associating' on the psychoanalyst's couch. I thought it permissible, for this difficult test case, to choose a compliant subject who yields himself easily and unconsciously".[15] In other words, like a model patient who delivers model material to his psychoanalyst. Sartre elaborates on this to an interviewer who posed the same question of why he chose Flaubert that he posed to himself: "Because he is the imaginary. With him, I am at the border, the barrier of dreams... It is clear that he detested himself, and when he speaks of his principle characters, he has a terrible attitude of sadism and masochism toward them: he tortures them because they are himself, and also to show that other people and the world torture him. He also tortures them because they are not him... In my book on Flaubert, I am studying imaginary persons - people who like Flaubert act out roles. A man is like a leak of gas, escaping into the imaginary. Flaubert did so perpetually; yet he also had to see reality because he hated it, so there is the whole question of the relationship between the real and the imaginary which I try to study in his life and work".[16] The style is pure Sartre; but the content of the answer is not too different from one that Freud might have given to a question about the challenge offered by his patients. In this vein, in another interview, Sartre also answers a question about the role he saw himself playing as a writer of literature that is not too different from the role of psychoanalyst that Freud invented: "A critical mirror. To show, to demonstrate, to represent... Once that's been done people have at least had a look at themselves; then they do what they want".[17]

Sartre never discusses the significance of approaching his biographical subjects as "case studies" in the psychoanalytic sense. With respect to clarifying their "bizarre qualities", however, they can be made coherent through a gloss on a small part of the work of the psychoanalyst Roy Schafer. Schafer's overall project, drawing from Sartre's work as well as others, is to purify the clinical language of psychoanalysis by cleansing it of its metapsychological baggage.[18] In the course of pursuing his project he addresses the problem of reconstructing a patient's life through the limits imposed by the psychoanalytic discourse. The problem faced by the psychoanalyst ever since Freud, is that the reconstruction of the patient's life depends on interpreting fragmentary material offered by the patient. This makes such reconstructions contingent on the psychoanalyst's interpretive frame of reference. As a result, "analysts with different points of view on theory and technique employ different narrative strategies, and so they develop analytic histories of different types and with more or less different content."[19] This is because "some interpretive answers concerning the past will not be based on, or seemingly, corroborated by content that is consciously remembered by the analysand".[20] The problem, of course, with reconstructing patients' histories that may not coincide with their memories, is that events that the analyst interprets as having happened in the patient's past may not have actually happened - precisely the kind of problem that Sartre's critics find him so notoriously casual about in his biographies.

Schafer seems about as casual and even indifferent to the problem as does Sartre. He reassures the analyst that although events in the patient's past may elude forever a faithful reconstruction, the past itself is not gone. "Because the reconstruction of the psychoanalytic past necessarily takes place in the here and now clinical dialogue, it remains an interpretable and reinterpretable feature of that here and now."[21] In other words, there is a sense in which the past is not gone but is alive and well in the transference and can be reconstructed through interpretation: "Reconstructions of the infantile past and the transferential present are interdependent... For example, present feelings of inadequacy direct the inquiry toward life-historical prototypes, and accounts of a never satisfied father direct the inquiry toward transference fantasies of a never satisfied analyst".[22] For the psychoanalyst, Schafer is arguing, the past that is alive in the transference is not the idea of a "past" limited to particular events involving the father, but the idea of a past involving patterns of relationship with the father. What is essential about a psychoanalytic reconstruction of the past are precisely those patterns of relationship that the patient lives in the present governed by his experience of the past. They are the material for a psychoanalytic understanding of a life history. The reconstruction of events involving the father may be heuristically useful for both patient and analyst, but it is not important that they be objectively true. While "these 'constructions in analysis' are required for the coherence, fallibility, and further development of the analytic life histories, and ideally they will withstand the challenge posed by alternative interpretations"[23], such an ideal is impossible to reach, since different interpretations based on radically different frames of reference can be contested endlessly. The burden of Schafer's argument is that it does not matter if events in a patient's past can be "objectively" known by the psychoanalyst, even those psychoanalysts who want to believe, like most biographers seem to, that particular events are causally related to patterns of relationships. The psychoanalyst's project for understanding a life is not a biographer's project but a therapist's project. For the psychoanalyst something may actually have happened in the past involving the father, but if it did, it is not important if it happened in one way or another, to paraphrase Sartre. The psychoanalyst's project is to clarify the patient's confusion over the meaning of the patterned relationships carried from the past through the present into the future so that he can recover himself as will, desire and in Sartre's case, freedom.

Sartre is following the logic of a therapist in reconstructing a life. Which is to say his biographies cannot be appreciated without appreciating the intimate connection to psychoanalysis that governs the evolution of his work. Sartre is not writing biographies of great writers, but psychoanalytic case studies that seize the therapeutic promise of psychoanalysis, and, as case studies are prone to do since Freud, extend that original therapeutic promise to the world. Sartre is not interested in understanding the events in his subject's past as if they were causal forces acting with a long reach. His interest is the psychoanalyst's interest in showing, representing, demonstrating, mirroring the enduring confusion his subjects experience about themselves so that we may see in their confusion our own. This much is true for Freud's cases, but Sartre's cases, unlike Freud's, move toward a vision of possibility which claims to complete psychoanalysis.

All of Sartre's cases have their theoretically supportive ground elsewhere in philosophical works which are a play between abstract ideas and concrete human experiences. The cases of Genet and Flaubert find their support in "The Critique of Dialectical Reason" and its so-called preface, "Search for a Method". Neither of these cases, however, fits as neatly into its theoretical support structures as "Baudelaire" does into "Being and Nothingness". "Baudelaire", in almost all respects, is a thin book because the ground that supports it has already been written in "Being and Nothingness". The book opens with a series of rhetorical questions. Baudelaire's life was a mass of contradictions he suffered, but "was his life really so alien to him? Supposing after all that he did deserve the life he had? Supposing that contrary to the accepted view, men always have the sort of lives they deserve?".[24] At the end, Sartre gives his answer already contained in his beginning: "It seems that in this life which was so closed and narrow, an accident or the intervention of chance would have enabled one to breathe...But we should look in vain for a single circumstance for which he was not fully and consciously responsible. Every event was a reflection of that indecomposable totality which he was from the first to the last day of his life. He refused experience. Nothing came from outside to change him and he learned nothing".[25]

This is not a simple judgment based on the thinnest reading of the idea that Baudelaire consciously chose his life. Sartre, after all, has already written an 800 page book on the complexity of this idea. What justifies "Being and Nothingness" is not only the idea that human beings are a "pure freedom" in the sense of freely and consciously choosing their lives, but that they do so deceiving themselves about what they are doing. "Baudelaire" is a case of confused experience about himself as the freedom which chooses its life. What he never learns is what he could have chosen to learn: that every human being is condemned to the judgment that he deserves his life because it is the nature of human beings to have no other nature than to be the being which inserts human reality into the world. "Being and Nothingness" is Sartre's project to understand the social bond through which every human subject deceives himself about the truth of his existence. His starting point is a radical view of subjectivity, which Merleau-Ponty summarizes as a "movement through which man is in the world and involves himself in a physical and social situation which then becomes his point of view on the world".[26]

In "Being and Nothingness" Sartre, without realizing it, is closer to Freud than to Freud's revisionists than in any of his subsequent works. Although the social bond is a constituent element in a subject's point of view on the world, in "Being and Nothingness" Sartre takes the subject's desires as his starting point for defining a human being. For Sartre as for Freud, human cultures institutionalize the social bond around a love of the highest sublime virtues which thinly disguises the violence they organize in the relationships between men. For Sartre, unlike Freud however, the movement of desire toward the social bond must always refer us to individual freedom. The problem with this is that it doesn't prove simple to say how the social bond can be changed from a way that humans deceive themselves about their freedom to the way they can realize their possibilities as the freedom which inserts human reality into the world. The problem becomes manifest in his presentation of Baudelaire's life.

Sartre begins his description of Baudelaire's life with a passive state of childhood innocence that precedes the activity of desire. He is describing Baudelaire's relationship to his mother which Sartre reconstructs from his lifelong fixation on her. Because we find something like this in Sartre's "Genet" and "Flaubert", but with a different meaning and significance between each of them, it is worth quoting in full:

> "Baudelaire was six when his father died. He worshipped his mother and was fascinated by her. He was surrounded by every care and comfort; he did not yet realize that he existed as a separate person, but felt that he was united body and soul to his mother in a primitive mystical relationship. He was submerged in the gentle warmth of their mutual love. There was nothing but a home, a family and an incestuous couple. 'I was always living in you,' he wrote to her in later life; 'you belonged to me alone. You were at once an idol and a friend.'

> "It would be impossible to improve upon his description of the sacred nature of their union. The mother was an idol, the child consecrated by her affection for him. Far from feeling that his existence was vague, aimless, superfluous, he thought of himself as son by divine right. He was always living in her which meant that he had found a sanctuary. He himself was nothing and did not want to be anything but an emanation of the divinity, a little thought which was always present in her mind. It was precisely because he was completely absorbed in a being who appeared to be a necessary being, to exist as of right, that he was

shielded from any feeling of disquiet, that he melted into the absolute and was justified".[27]

It seems like a beginning, but we cannot make too much of it. It is not a true beginning. Baudelaire's mother does not represent the absent which defines Baudelaire's desires that give rise to the project identical to his life. True, Sartre quotes him as speaking of her in terms suggesting that his fixation on his mother is a classical expression of the Oedipus Complex. "His mother's second marriage" Sartre observes, "was the one event in his life he could not accept. He was inexhaustible on the subject, and his terrible logic always summed it up in these words: 'When one has a son like me' - 'like me' was understood - 'one doesn't remarry'".[28] But Baudelaire was deceiving himself about what his mother represented for him. It was not his mother he desired, but the justification for his life which he experienced through her before he experienced himself as the activity of desire that would carry him into his life. "One moment" Sartre tells us "he was still enveloped in the communal religious life of the couple consisting of his mother and himself; the next life had gone out like a tide leaving him high and dry. The justification for his existence had disappeared; he made the mortifying discovery that he was a single person, that his life had been given him for nothing. His rage at being driven out was colored by a profound sense of having fallen from grace".[29] The beginning of existence is actually the beginning of a life, and existence begins with what Sartre often refers to in the abstract discussions in "Being and Nothingness" as an "upsurge of consciousness" into the world, but which, in referring to the concrete event that begins Baudelaire's life, he describes as consciousness falling into the absolute emptiness of itself that constitutes it as desire whose object is to fill that emptiness with itself. Both consciousness as intention, and desire as the experience of absence, arise coevally in "Being and Nothingness", supported only by themselves, and never referring to objects in the world that would define desire in the conventional sense as "need". Existence begins not with desire constituted as need moving toward the objects of the world that can satisfy it, but as a falling away from the world which is what makes existence, in "Being and Nothingness," precisely and exactly identical to freedom as nothingness.

Freedom arises in the world as a fall into "a cleavage between the immediate psychic past and the present...This cleavage is precisely nothingness"[30] and nothingness is precisely what is meant by freedom. Freedom upsurges into the world as a fall into an absolute and pure lack of being which experiences the world constituted for it as a stage on which it can play a plenitude of possible beings it can cause itself to be by choosing relationships to the plenitude of other beings that occupy the world. In "Baudelaire" Sartre feels that no one has described the moment at which existence begins "better than Hughes in 'A High Wind in Jamaica'".[31] He quotes the scene when, as Hughes writes it, "it suddenly flashed into [Emily's] mind that she was *she*...What agency had so ordered it that out of all the people in the world who she might have been, she was this particular one, this Emily: born in such and such a year out of all the Years in Time...Had she chosen it herself, or had God done it?...Wasn't she perhaps God, herself?". [32]

For Sartre, "this lightning intuition is completely empty. The child has just acquired the conviction that she is just not anyone, but it is precisely by acquiring this conviction that she becomes just anyone. She feels, to be sure, that she is someone different than the others, but each of the others has the same feeling of being different from everyone else. The child has undergone a purely negative experience of separation and her experience assumes the form of universal subjectivism - a sterile form which Hegel defined by the equation I=I".[33] The fall into the world is a fall that simultaneously invests freedom with power and condemns it to the powerlessness of pursuing a being it chooses to be to escape itself as a sterile emptiness which it can never escape being. Freedom cannot be defined as a need constituted by a particular object; nevertheless freedom "participates in the necessity which prescribes that consciousness be consciousness *of* something... Freedom is the freedom of choosing but not the freedom of not choosing".[34] What freedom must choose is the being it desires to be even though it can never be other than a being "always engaged... as a choice in the making".[35] We all know Sartre's formula: "Man is a useless passion"; the freedom which flees its being as freedom toward being a being that it has unconditionally chosen to be the cause and foundation of itself,[36] which is another way of saying to be God.[37] Freedom's upsurge into the world is best described as a fall into an awareness that one is absolutely bereft of the power to be God and must live as the absolute powerlessness of freedom to be the being it chooses to be. In other words, consciousness' fall into itself as nothingness is a fall into the awareness of its condition that it can be the cause but not the foundation of the being it must choose itself to be, because it must found that being on a pattern of relationships to other beings just like itself. That is why Emily's revelation about her separateness, again in Hughes' description which Sartre quotes, is followed by "a sudden terror...Did anyone know? (Know, I mean, that she was someone in particular, Emily - perhaps even God - not just any little girl.) She could not tell why, but the idea terrified her... At all costs she must hide *that* from them."[38] Perhaps Emily is God, but if she is, it is also true for everyone else who is like her. Sartre betrays how little he wanted to understand Freud's work by not seeing that in Freud, as in "Being and Nothingness", the primordial "point of view on the world" which governs individual lives, and hence the life of the world, is a Hobbesian like terror. No doubt this misreading of Freud was essential to his own ambition to make psychoanalysis his own by supplying it with the right theory to complete it. This ambition, which drives his entire work, begins in "Being and Nothingness" with a dramatically presented difference between himself and Freud. If the Oedipus complex is the master metaphor governing Freud's psychoanalysis, then the master metaphor in Sartre's existential psychoanalysis is the "Actaeon complex".[39] The pursuit of being is a hunt that defines the project of every human life. "Does anyone know?" is Emily's terror; her desire is to know herself with the certainty that endows the self with the density and solidity of Being. This kind of knowledge of the self, however, is a secret buried in the world which must be appropriated from the world. "What is seen is possessed; to see is to deflower." Freedom must violate the world in pursuit of its being, and incur the risk of being violated. "If we examine the comparisons ordinarily used to express the relation between the knower and the known, we see that many of them are represented as being a kind of *violation by sight*. The unknown object is given as immaculate, as virgin, comparable to a *whiteness*. It has not yet 'delivered up' its secret; man has not yet 'snatched' its secret away from it... Every investigation implies the idea of a nudity which one brings out into the open by clearing away the obstacles that cover it, just as Actaeon clears away the branches so that he can have a better view of Diana at her bath... Knowledge is a hunt. Bacon called it the hunt of Pan".[40]

While the Actaeon complex is meant to be differentiated from the Oedipus Complex, it is still a complex in Freud's original sense. "Baudelaire's fundamental attitude" writes Sartre, "was that of a man bending over himself - bending over his own reflection like Narcissus".[41] The "narcissistic attitude" is freedom's hunt for itself as a useless passion. Baudelaire lives his life imprisoned in the Actaeon complex which makes his life a false history - an empty repetition with no movement. Sartre's term "passion" is judiciously chosen on two grounds: first it conveys a suffering which, although self imposed, freedom is condemned to bear by being condemned to take its own self as the object of its desires. Second, since passion is always a love story, it casts the kind of suspicion on love which surrounds Freud's work with controversy. The useless pursuit of one's being must be mediated by possessing the being of the other who is the foundation of the being freedom causes itself to be. Loving another is for Sartre, at the beginning of his work, the kind of possessive act whose prototype Freud saw in the transference love of the patient. Iris Murdoch is correct in her critical observation that in "Being and Nothingness", Sartre treats love in a "curiously abstract" manner - as "a craving which is frustrated because of the reciprocal nature of the demand and because of the loneliness and essential poverty of the imagination...There is no suggestion in Sartre's account that love is connected with action and day-to-day living; that it is other than a battle between two hypnotists in a closed room".[42] Love, in "Being and Nothingness", is no more accorded the status of a primordial experience than it is anywhere in Freud's work. It only has the status of disguising what is primordial - freedom's struggle with itself to escape into the density of being from what it is condemned to be, nothing but freedom. Love, which never dreams anything but serious dreams, is what allows freedom to take its useless passion seriously, as if it could find a final solution to its struggles. While in Freud the secondary, derivative status of love never varies, by the time Sartre is analyzing the case of Flaubert, the status of love, as we shall see, changes to that of a primordial experience, the status that all of Freud's revisionists are eager to accord it. In "Being and Nothingness" Sartre insists on putting love everywhere under the sign of suspicion. Under that sign he introduces the problem of the deceived consciousness as the problem of self deception which justifies his psychoanalytic project.

The problem of self deception has never stopped being debated in philosophy. There the problem is usually defined in terms of the paradox of a self-deceiver who believes in p and tries to deceive himself that he believes in non-p, which, of course, implies a prior awareness of p.[43] Neither Freud's work nor Sartre's enters the debate on how to solve the paradox. In Freud the problem simply dissolves as the primacy of the subject dissolves until "self-deception is nowhere, because the mechanisms that explain denial, or repression, or the censorship of unconscious material do not represent the activities of *the self...* One subsystem systematically misleads others".[44] In Sartre, self-deception never involves deception about a belief. Freedom is not a belief, but a way in which a subject experiences himself situated in the world in pursuit of his being. In "Being and Nothingness", anguish is the experience of freedom. Anguish is an emotion which is unlike any other emotion. Sartre, Fell points out, does not think of emotions as "superventions" in the sense of acting on passive individuals.[45] "In this respect emotion is no different from other types of activities".[46] Sartre carries into "Being and Nothingness" his views on emotion which he presents in his earlier work on "The Emotions". The concept of "emotions" refers us to an "emotional consciousness" of something which signifies the intentions of consciousness. In a way, emotions are like a coloration added to the meanings of the world which signify intentions to transform "by magic" an "urgent and difficult world" in which "all the ways are barred".[47] Anguish, however, is a privileged emotion in that, unlike the other emotions, it does not refer us to a subject's intentional acts, but to the freedom of the subject who acts. "Kierkegaard is right" Sartre tells us in "Being and Nothingness", "anguish is distinguished from fear in that fear is fear of beings in the world, whereas anguish is anguish before myself." Anguish is a form of knowledge that consciousness has of itself as freedom. "Anguish is a specific consciousness of freedom..."; anguish is freedom disclosing its being to itself.[48]

This disclosure, and not particular beliefs, is what self-deception is about, although beliefs play a role in self-deception. While the subject cannot deceive himself about experiencing anguish, he can deceive himself about the truth of that experience by hiding that truth in a belief about it. Believing is a project of constructing, to use Fingarette's helpful term, a "cover story"[49] to conceal the experience of anguish as one which presents the subject to himself as freedom. This is why Sartre calls self-deception throughout "Being and Nothingness" an act of "bad faith". Believing embeds anguish in a "cover story" that positions another as the condition that distances the subject from being the being he pursues which he knows he is already. Baudelaire's passion for being a self does not disguise his anguish, but justifies it by disguising the impossibility of his catching his quarry. Condemned as freedom to be only a "deformed image" of himself[50], his passion takes the form of what Sartre, in his later work, characterizes as the game of "loser-wins". From the outside, Baudelaire's life appears like a great rebellion which, like all rebellions, starts by tasting its victory. It is a rebellion which opposes being consigned to a destiny of being a deformed self. Baudelaire begins his life like "the child who has become aware of himself as a separate being with a sense of despair, rage and jealousy". This child "will base his whole life on the fruitless contemplation of a singularity which is formal. 'You threw me out' he will say to his parents. 'You threw me out of the perfect whole of which I was part and condemned me to a separate existence. Well now I am going to turn this existence against you. If you ever wanted to get me back again, it would be impossible because I have become conscious of myself as separate from and against everybody else.' And he will say to his school fellows and the street urchins who persecute him: 'I'm someone else, someone different from all of you who are responsible for all of my sufferings. You can persecute my body but you can't touch my otherness.' This assertion is both a claim and a gesture of defiance. He is someone else, and because he is someone else he is out of reach and already almost revenged on his oppressors". [51]

"Almost" is a gulf that can never be bridged. Baudelaire dreams of crossing it by becoming that singular unique self he believes was stolen from him by those who exiled him into nothingness. Baudelaire's beginning is a confused experience over "the *not*, as an abrupt intuitive discovery..."[52] which arises from our falling into the world. "The necessary condition for our saying *not* is that non-being be a perpetual presence in us and outside of us, that nothingness haunt being".[53] If existence requires filling a sterile empty nothingness with a positivity that enables it to be lived as a project, then Baudelaire fills it with the concrete positivity of a drama of passionate revenge whose possibility lies in appropriating for himself the destiny consigned to him, in order to reverse the order of mirror and image. His cover story is all fantasy, the delirium of everyday life.

Sartre never uses the term "transference", possibly because it would imply he was too much a captive of psychoanalysis, when it was he who wanted to play the role of captor. Baudelaire's life, however, unfolds as another version of the transference. Sartre's reconstruction of Baudelaire's life, LaCapra points out, depicts him as "only a rebel and not a revolutionary. His attitude was parasitic upon the status quo, which he needed for his own poses and role playing".[54] For Sartre, it is a question of describing his fall into parasitism at the beginning: "He was trying to discover his own *nature*, that is to say his character and his being, but all he saw was the long, monotonous procession of his states of mind. He grew exasperated. He perceived so clearly what constituted the singularity of General Aupick or of his mother. Why then should he be deprived of the private enjoyment of his own originality?".[55] Baudelaire is a parasite which, unlike his biological counterpart, and like the patient in the scene of the transference, intends to keep his host alive. From the beginning there are poses and role playing waiting to come onstage. "We can see already that with Mme. Aupick he was anxious to pose as a victim. The letters that he wrote to her are a curious mixture of confession and disguised reproach... The first was to assuage his rancor - he wanted his mother to feel remorse. The second was more complex. Mme. Aupick represented the judge, represented Good. In her presence he humiliated himself and sought simultaneously condemnation and absolution. But he both hated and respected this Good which he maintained forcibly like a screen in front of him. He hated it because it curbed his freedom, because he had chosen it precisely so that it would be a curb. Those standards were there *in order to be violated*, but they were also there to arouse remorse in the person who violated them".[56]

Similar to Freud's "Rat Man" and "Wolf Man", Baudelaire is imprisoned in the game of "loser-wins". The game depends on what Sartre calls, in "Being and Nothingness", an "attitude of seriousness" which hypostatizes value as an untranscendable basis for the given order of things. "The spirit of seriousness has two characteristics: it considers values as transcendent given independent of human subjectivity, and it transfers the quality of 'desirable' from the ontological structure of things to their simple material constitution. For the spirit of seriousness, for example, *bread* is desirable because it is *necessary* to live (a value written in an intelligible heaven) and because bread *is* nourishing. The result of the serious attitude, which as we know rules the world, is to cause the symbolic values of things to be drunk in by their empirical idiosyncrasy as ink by a blotter; it puts forward the opacity of the desired object and posits it in itself as a desirable irreducible".[57]

Sartre's interpretation of Baudelaire's life as a history of self-deception is saturated through and through with the psychoanalytic promise that Baudelaire can do a work of consciousness that will cure him of his bad faith so that he can live his life as the possibility of freedom. What possibility is that? Sartre provides an answer of sorts: "Baudelaire is an ethics which is ashamed of itself and does not dare speak its name".[58] This is an answer, in fact, which cannot speak its own name. It annunciates freedom recovering itself from bad faith by subordinating itself to the commands of a value that bonds it to others. The paradox which this vision of possibility expresses for defining freedom cannot be said to have eluded Sartre. Nevertheless, in accord with his consuming passion to oppose the cunning deceits of bad faith wherever he finds them with a univocal language that will function in LaCapra's terms, "as a primary voice, pure of the dangers of ambiguity, multivalent meaning, and figurative usage..."[59] he allows the paradox to carry him to his famous last word in "Being and Nothingness". Like Freud's, this is a famous last word that settles nothing: "What are we to understand by this being which wills to hold itself in awe, to be at a distance from itself? Is it a question of bad faith or of another fundamental attitude? And can one *live* this new aspect of being? In particular will freedom by taking itself for an end escape all *situation*? Or on the contrary will it remain situated? Or will it situate itself so much the more precisely and the more individually as it projects itself further in anguish as a conditioned freedom and accepts more fully its responsibility as an existent by whom the world comes into being? All these questions... can find their reply only on the ethical plane. We shall devote to them a future work".[60]

Sartre never writes that future work. How could he? The confusing questions which it would presumably answer are less like a prologue to such a work than a confession that "Being and Nothingness" has settled nothing about the definition of a subject as freedom. Sartre's call to Baudelaire to dare speak an ethics as his possibility is not in accord with the sudden lucidity, like a lightening bolt, that accompanies his fall into the world as freedom, as it does Emily's, illuminating in its pitiless light that there is nothing in the world to which value can be affixed in an enduring way as if it were a label pasted onto the things of the world. There is much yet to be done to reformulate a radically pure definition of freedom as an absolute emptiness resting on no foundation but itself, with no nucleus to govern its relations to the world, into a freedom that can recover and live its possibilities as freedom by living the terms of a social bond commanded by values.

"Being and Nothingness" has a fulcrum imminent in its arguments for levering one definition of freedom into the other. In "Being and Nothingness" Sartre places horror on the side of the world as if the world were a mirror revealing consciousness to itself as a freedom which needs but cannot want the world. "What we must do" Sartre writes as the opening sentence for his section on *Quality as a Revelation of Being*, "is to attempt a psychoanalysis of things." In attempting to understand how we experience the things of the world, the "term *imagination* does not suit us and neither does that attempt to look behind things and their gelatinous, solid or fluid matter, for the images which we project there...Of course the 'human' meaning of *sticky*, of *slimy*, etc. does not belong to the in-itself. But potentialities do not belong to it either... and yet it is these which constitute the world. Material meanings, the human sense of needles, snow, grained wood, of crowded, of greasy etc. are as real as the world, neither more nor less, and to come into the world means to rise up in the midst of these meanings".[61] We are being prepared for a long and in many ways unparalleled presentation of the meaning of the experience of the "slimy", to be followed by one on the "hole". The meaning of the "slimy" cannot be reduced to a matter of "projection". Such an explanation makes "sliminess proper, considered in its isolated state... not *repugnant*... There would have to be a kind of apprenticeship for learning the symbolic value of 'slimy'. But observation teaches us that even very young children show evidence of repulsion in the presence of something slimy, as if it were already combined with the psychic".[62]

Sartre's problematic appeal to empirical evidence notwithstanding, the world reveals that "the slimy is *myself*, by the very fact that I outline an appropriation of the slimy substance".[63] The meaning of the slimy lies in my struggle with it. The slimy "symbolizes the resistance of my being to absorption into the in-itself... The slimy offers a horrible image; it is horrible in itself for a consciousness to become slimy... The horror of the slimy is the horrible fear that time might become slimy, that facticity might progress continually and insensibly and absorb the For-itself which *exists* it. It is not the fear of death, not of the pure in-itself, not of nothingness, but of a particular type of being, which does not actually exist any more than the In-itself-For-itself and which is only *represented* by the slimy. It is an ideal being which I reject with all my strength and which haunts me as *value* haunts my being, an ideal being in which the foundationless In-itself has priority over the For-itself. We shall call it an *Antivalue*".64

The "Other" who is like me, is the anti-value against which freedom struggles. The horror of the world falls on the side of the world. "I need the Other in order to realize fully all the structures of my being".65 At the same time the appearance of the Other is troped as a hole in the meaning that freedom has inserted into the world that is the world for which freedom is responsible. The appearance of "the Other is first the permanent flight of things toward a goal which I apprehend as an object at a certain distance from me but which escapes me inasmuch as it unfolds about itself its own distances... The appearance of the Other in the world corresponds therefore to a fixed sliding of the whole universe, to a decentralization of the world which undermines the centralization which I am simultaneously effecting... we are not dealing here with a flight of the world toward nothingness or outside itself. Rather it appears that the world has a kind of drain hole in the middle of its being and that it is perpetually flowing off through this hole. The universe, the flow and the drain hole are all once again recovered, reapprehended and fixed as an object. All this is there *for me* as a partial structure of the world, even though the total disintegration of the universe is involved". 66

There is more implied by this about Emily's terror than the awareness that burst upon her that she was "a distinct person". What is implied is the possibility of rethinking her life and Baudelaire's, as beginning not with a fall into the empty sterility of freedom but with a fall into a struggle with the horror of the world represented as "anti-value". We can read the concept of "anti-value" as if it were an invitation waiting to be accepted by the one who issued it to rethink the entire tripartite relationship between human beings, consciousness and freedom which "Being and Nothingness" adumbrates. It is only a question of historicizing the horror already put on the side of the world, and inserting history into freedom as its nucleus. What we would then have is the making of a coherent story about a subject denied by history the realization of his possibilities as freedom, rather than a story about a subject denied his possibilities by being a freedom which has no possibilities. This latter story lacks coherency because recovery from the self-deceptions that cripple a life cannot be thought. Without the possibility of a last word that is a vision of possibility, "Being and Nothingness" and "Baudelaire" collapse into the incoherency of stories that need never have been told. It doesn't matter whether freedom recovers itself as freedom, it must pursue the useless passion of being the self it chooses to be if it is not to be swept into the hole of the world as a horror. Bad faith is the illusion freedom must live as its possibility, whether it knows it or not, if it is not to lose its struggle to push off the impossible horror of being absorbed into the horror of the world.

At the same time that nothing is settled in "Being and Nothingness", everything waits to be settled. The movement in Sartre's work toward the last word that fails in "Being and Nothingness" follows the star of his never ending love affair with the idea of consciousness as a work of freedom recovering itself from the delirium of a false consciousness. Sartre's case presentation of Genet is the Rubicon which Sartre crosses in his pursuit of the last word. Genet's beginning, unlike Baudelaire's, contains its end. "In Sartre's view, Genet achieved something of the equivalent of a psychoanalytic cure."[67] Sartre presents Genet's life, unlike Baudelaire's, as a disordered possibility measured by a real possibility that, from the beginning, is what freedom struggles to realize.

*

With "Genet", Sartre enters the revisionist scene of reading Freud. Genet struggles with a world which, in violating its own possibilities, violates Genet's possibilities. In Genet, as Laing and Cooper note, "the wicked man is the invention of the good man... All evil for Sartre is projection".[68] As Sartre puts it, the "function" of the other defined as evil for those who define the other as evil "is to take their forbidden desires upon himself and to reflect them like a mirror". The victim "must incorporate these desires into himself, must internalize them, must make them *his* desires".[69] Anguish, now has a source and a reason unlike in "Being and Nothingness" where it is the subject present to himself as freedom. Anguish, wearing a new face as a wound called "alienation" delivered by the world, now plays the role of nemesis filling the distance between the subject and the world he struggles toward to realize his possibilities.

Psychoanalysis itself is assigned a new role in understanding the history of the self as alienation. Existential psychoanalysis, which in "Being and Nothingness" was meant to complete Freud's ambition to separate psychoanalysis from everything in its provenance, is now part of a troika of lovers of the truth that promises freedom's freedom. The relationship between existentialism and psychoanalysis which once stood as a method without a theory is reconfigured so that psychoanalysis finds its theory in Marxist theory, positioned alongside a number of "auxiliary disciplines". Existentialism is not one of them. In a monumental act of bad faith, Sartre humbles himself by calling it "a parasitical system living on the margin of Knowledge, which at first it opposed but into which today it seeks to be integrated".[70] In reality, of course, Sartre intends just the opposite. The last word that renders struggle coherent with a vision of possibility privileged from suspicion must always be based on the Real. History, which is always struggle in motion, can be made coherent only by assuming an absolutely fixed point of vantage. The Real belongs to Marx, who supplies it with a framework of history within which subjects can reach for their freedom, but the vision of possibility belongs to Sartre who supplies it with a psychoanalytic theory that defines the subject as freedom.

Genet's freedom is no longer an anguished nothingness opposed to the plenitude of materiality that makes up the horror of the world, but is itself a form of materiality which must work the materiality of the world to realize its possibilities. Genet may be a writer, but writing is a form of labor, and the writer's struggles share their meaning with the struggles of other laborers. Sartre's definition of the individual subject as freedom follows Marx to catch up with Darwin and be captured by him; just the reverse of Freud who is entangled with Darwin at the beginning and devotes himself to disentangling from him. In the "Critique of Dialectical Reason", Sartre instructs us to "see what is the real rationality of action, at the level of individual *praxis*...Everything is to be explained through *need (le besoin)*; need is the first totalizing relation between the material being, man, and the material ensemble of which he is a part".[71] Before human desire knows itself as desire it is lack formed by the invisible hand of the Law of Survival. "Need is a link of *univocal imminence* with surrounding materiality insofar as the organism *tries to sustain itself* with it... In effect, a biological statute is superimposed in the organism, on a physico-chemical statute".[72] Whether these statutes imposed and superimposed on the level of organismic life are meant to refer us to the operations of the same dialectical law that governs human history is no clearer in Sartre than in Marx and Engels. What is clear is that the dialectical movement of history - totalizations, detotalizations and retotalizations - cannot be thought without first thinking "the living body... *in danger* in the universe, and the universe harbors the possibility of the *non-being* of the organism. Conversely, if it is to find its being within Nature or to protect itself against destruction, the organic totality must transform itself into inert matter, for it is only as a mechanical system that it can modify the material environment. The man of need is an organic totality perpetually making itself into its own tool in the milieu of exteriority".[73] But a machine tool is precisely what a human being cannot be. Need governed by the law of survival is the negation which sets into motion life as human life. "The *project*, as transcendence, is merely the exteriorization of imminence; transcendence itself is already present in the functional fact of nutrition and excretion..."[74] Sartre is no longer interested in the radical question that Freud asks: Why do human beings everywhere identify their lives with the life of their society? Put another way, what is the meaning of society to human beings who everywhere love it? Marx relieves Sartre of the burden of these questions. The necessity for survival brings human beings into concerted action with each other. The theoretical context for Genet is that society is simply the exteriorization of the human project imminent in being an organism with needs. "The meaning of labor is provided *by an end*, and need, far from being a *vis a tergo* pushing the laborer, is in fact the lived revelation of a goal to aim at, and this goal is, in the first instance, simply the restoration of the organism. Eventually, action really converts the material surroundings into a real whole on the basis of which an organisation of means to an end is possible".[75] Freedom as need guarantees the intersubjective world because freedom has no identity except as part of an organized system of praxes we call human society. Keeping in mind that Genet's writing is a form of labor, we then have Genet born into a world in which to consider *an individual* at work is a complete abstraction, since in reality labor is as much a relation between men as a relation between man and the material world.[76]

The social system of organized labor moves as a dialectical history exteriorizing itself at different times "in a particular and contingent form since the whole of human development, at least up to now, has been a bitter struggle against *scarcity*".[77] It is the fact of scarcity that shapes the historical forms of the bitter struggle between man and the material world into a bitter struggle between men: "Each (man) refuses to serve the Other's end and, while recognising his own objective being as a means within the adversary's project, he uses his own instrumentality *in others* to make them an instrument of his own ends in spite of themselves. This is *struggle*; in it, everyone reduces himself to his materiality so as to act on that of the Other; through pretences, stratagems, frauds and maneuvers everyone allows himself to be constituted by the Other as a *false object, a deceptive means*".[78] The hunt of Actaeon for being is now the hunt of being for survival written large on the social stage of history as the rape men commit in concert with each other on each other in a struggle against scarcity. Within this larger story of history, the story of Genet's history unfolds as the struggle of the victim. And since each man struggling against the Other in a struggle against scarcity is not human destiny, the end, unlike the case of Baudelaire, is contained in Genet's beginning.

Genet, like Baudelaire, begins his life with a shattered innocence: as "an accident [which] riveted him to a childhood memory, and this memory became sacred...he knew paradise and lost it, he was a child and was driven from his childhood".[79]

The riveting moment is not the same for Genet as it is for Baudelaire. Genet, the foundling, is playing alone in the kitchen experiencing the anxiety of his solitude. "So he 'absented' himself ... He plunged into a kind of ecstasy... an abandoned consciousness reflecting... utensils. A drawer is opening; a little hand moves forward. *Caught in the act...* A voice declares publicly: 'you're a thief', The child is ten years old. That was how it happened, in that or some other way".[80] The event is not the same as Baudelaire's but its results are the same. "Genet carries in his heart a bygone instant which has lost none of its virulence, an infinitesmal and sacred void which concludes a death and begins a horrible metamorphosis." What it sets into motion is the same. Out of the horror of a shattered innocence arises a life lived as a "liturgical drama... A child dies of shame; a hoodlum rises up in his place; the hoodlum will be haunted by the child".[81] The moment of negativity is transformed for both Baudelaire and Genet into the positivity of a life lived as a struggle against a destiny conferred on them to be exiles from life. Both live this life as a refusal of this destiny; a refusal which imprisons them in the game of loser-wins. There is, however, a small but perceptible difference in their beginning, which is the difference that makes all the difference. While Sartre never pursues it in "Genet", it is like a small trace that anticipates the theme he is to elaborate in "Flaubert". The foundling Genet is anxious over his solitude, feels bereft of the identity of belonging *before the Fall*. Baudelaire begins by falling into a world he needs as the foundation of his being, but cannot want because it is purely and simply another name for unsurpassable horror. Genet, on the other hand, begins longing for the world he needs before the fatal instant in which he encounters it as a horror that consigns him to the destiny of being a horror. Before the fall, Genet's lived experience which governs the trajectory of his life has, at its heart, a knowledge he does not know he possesses: he both needs and wants the world which is to exile him. His possibilities depend on changing the world as well as himself.

The end is already in the beginning: the end waits for Genet's discovery that from the beginning he has been the freedom which needs and wants a world in which he can realize his possibilities. In Genet, it is a question of "discovery" rather than a "recovery" of something lost. While Sartre speaks of a fall in Genet, the moment at which Genet is called a thief is not really a fall. There is no "Eden-like" innocence that precedes it. There is only a kind of innocent passivity which already has at its center the malevolent activity of alienation. In the beginning is the lived experience of freedom dependent on the world. Genet must begin his life bonded to a knowledge that knows him as an object before he can know himself. In this way Sartre wants us to see Genet as no different than any child born into a society totalized by capitalist values. "Grownups never weary taking stock of their belongings: this is called regarding. The child is part of the lot, between two stools or under the table. He comes to know himself through their regard, and his happiness lies in being part of the stock. To Be is to belong to someone. If property defines Being, the quiet, sober steadiness of earthly possessions defines the Good".[82] In another way, we must see Genet, the bastard foundling who "has neither mother nor heritage"[83] as unlike other children, an object without a provenance. As a result, from the beginning, he "lives in a state of uneasiness. The pious and lawful vocables which he has been made to learn are not quite applicable to what he is and what he feels. But as he possesses no others, he can neither describe nor define his malaise... Yet it expresses his deepest reality, which is contradictory, for his self certainty contradicts the truth that he is for others".[84] So it must be with freedom in the beginning: it must know itself first as a specular image reflected by others. At the same time, it knows through a different kind of knowledge, that it can never live the experience of itself as an object because it is freedom. The fateful moment at which Genet is publicly called a thief is the moment at which the dormant freedom that he is arises to become active as his life. This resistance is the small excess of freedom which struggles with its own desires identified with another's desires that first define the subject. Resistance, unlike in Freud, is moved to the margins of the story of an individual's development because the individual is at the center of the story. Resistance is given its proper position in a narrative in which everything is settled.

The life Genet begins to live as a subject who must objectivize himself in the world through the mediation of others, centers on a struggle with the horror of the other conferring on him the destiny of being a horror. Genet begins needing and wanting the world, but "is the victim of a cruel hoax".[85] The world is the Good which destines him never to belong to the Good. He is labelled, like an object, an evil thief, and "he affirms the priority of the object which he is to them over the subject which he is to himself".[86] But if Genet, exiled from the world cannot want to live his life wanting the world in order to be, what can he want? He will live his life as a passion to bring himself into being by moving away from the world rather than toward it. "First of all he wants to escape his destiny." He will pursue totalizing himself as the unacceptable he has been consigned to be - he will merge himself "with the substantial being of the Evildoer or the Thief".[87] By seizing for himself the destiny conferred on him by others, he will reverse the order of mirror and image, making the unacceptable the totally acceptable. "In short, he learns to think the unthinkable, to maintain the unmaintainable, to pose as true what he very well knows to be false...He will build a whole system of sophistry on this procedure and that he will one day be able to turn it against the flabbergasted right-thinking man".[88] This system of sophistry is the beginning of Genet's life lived as the game of loser-wins. Genet, however, is not Baudelaire. Genet is not only struggling to realize his passion - to "be his own fatality", to "live this impossibility of living as if he had created it expressly for himself," to "try to love" a destiny he has willed[89] - he is struggling against his passion. Sartre traces the "whirligigs" and double binds that constitute the cunning tactics Genet pursues in his struggles with a psychoanalytic perspicacity that exceeds most analyses of a patient's transference, including Freud's. Sartre's case history of Genet's life, stretching over five hundred pages, is too dense, too abstract, and too rich to summarize. It is a history that Sartre constructs guided by the movement of Genet's struggle to leave his passion behind. Genet's life is a dialectical movement of totalizations detotalized and retotalized which has the shape of a gyre that rotates around an axis pointing toward Genet's desires becoming transparent to himself. The movement of Genet's life from the darkness to the light is the discovery that he is a freedom which needs and wants the world as its possibility.

Sartre's case of Genet follows the plot of revisionist narratives calculated to complete Freud. It has the mythic qualities of a journey from the limitlessness of the Imaginary to the humbling discovery of the limits of the Real, constituted as a vision of human possibility. Sartre gives this vision of possibility a powerful image which he attaches to himself as the last words in his "autobiography", "The Words": "If I relegate impossible Salvation to the proproom, what remains? A whole man, composed of all men and as good as all of them and no better than any".[90] Genet's journey is mapped by Sartre's journey toward an awakening from the illusion of Salvation. "Culture doesn't save anything or anyone, it doesn't justify. But it's a product of man: he projects himself into it, he recognizes himself in it; that critical mirror alone offers him his image".[91] In brief, we begin our lives born under the sign of chance; but chance does not rule the world. We are the Beings who are privileged to make something out of what is given to us; freedom is the name for that privilege and society the name for its possibility. Sartre, at the end of "The Words" presents himself as cured: "I have changed. I shall speak later on about the acids that corroded the distorting transparencies which enveloped me; I shall tell when and how I served my apprenticeship to violence and discovered my ugliness - which for a long time was my negative principle, the quicklime in which the wonderful child was dissolved; I shall also explain the reason why I came to think systematically against myself, to the extent of measuring the obvious truth of an idea by the displeasure it caused me. The retrospective illusion has been smashed to bits; martyrdom, salvation, and immortality are falling to pieces; the edifice is going to wrack and ruin..."[92] It would be hard to find a better description of the cure the psychoanalytic patient is expected to perform in that compressed space Freud called the "transference". Sartre who is not a foundling bastard like Genet, maps Genet's project with his own life, beginning with the status of an exile conferred by the paternal bond, passing through the violent pursuit of an end to reverse the order of mirror and image toward a final end that leaves that violent project behind for a vision of possibility. How could Sartre not map it with his own life? The coherency of every life that begins within the compass of the same historical moment depends on the same story. It does not matter if the final end is reached or not, because no one who is a human being can escape the end contained in its beginning. The ending presented in "The Words" strikes a note of solitude. It is not the ontological note in "Being and Nothingness" of a solitary freedom which cannot escape itself as freedom sunk into the hole of the solitude which defines it. It is rather an anticipatory note for a vision of possibility of a world in which beings who are free not only need each other as beings in order to be, but want each other to be free in order for each to be freedom. This world has yet to be made, but its possibility as a vision of human possibility is carried by each human's discovery of himself as a whole man who cannot think himself without thinking that other whole men in the world are part of him. This is Genet's discovery at the end of his violent and tortuous journey.

First Genet must "reach the point of planning *to make himself understood*, a radical conversion of his attitude toward others is required; and even that is not enough; he must relearn to speak".[93] This is what it means for Genet to have labored at becoming a writer. Referring to Genet's "Our Lady of the Flowers", Sartre states that "this work is, without the author's suspecting it, the journal of a detoxification, of a conversion. In it Genet detoxicates himself of himself and turns to the outside world".[94] In it "Genet shows everything. Since his only aim is to please himself, he sets down everything". More is involved than self-pleasure. "By the same movement that chains him, in his work, to these drifting, rudderless creatures, he frees himself, shakes off his reverie and transforms himself into a creator. *Our Lady* is a dream that contains its own awakening."[95]

Freud could not have expressed more vividly the original promise which justifies psychoanalysis but which he failed to deliver. "By infecting us with his evil, Genet delivers himself from it. Each of his books is a cathartic attack of possession, a psychodrama; in appearance each of them merely repeats the preceding one, as his new love affairs repeat the old: but with each work he masters increasingly the demon that possesses him. His ten years of literature are equivalent to a psychoanalytic cure".[96] Like a patient who senses that his psychoanalysis is nearly over, "he hastens toward the moment when he will write 'THE END' at the bottom of the last page and when he will have *nothing more to say* because he will have *said everything*".[97] Having said everything Genet then knows everything, fulfilling the revisionist dream of the ideal psychoanalytic patient. Genet, saying everything, discovers the illusions that have trapped his life in a contradiction that goes nowhere. "This contradiction reflected his own conflict: society had to welcome him *as he was*, that is *as an evildoer*. But is not the evildoer the man whom all society rejects? It therefore had to glorify him precisely to the extent that it condemned him".[98] Sartre can give Genet's life a coherency he could not give Baudelaire's, because he can envision Genet transcending what trapped Baudelaire forever : a "form of pride [that] is as unhappy as it is pure because it revolves in the void and feeds on itself".[99] Genet discovers that he is the transcendental activity of freedom by which a human makes something different out of what is given him. He is a whole human who faces a world of other whole humans as his possibility. It is a humbling experience, but that is what possibility is: "One must will an act to the very end. But the act is alive, it changes. The goal one sets at the beginning is abstract and consequently false. Little by little it is enriched by the means employed to attain it, and ultimately the concrete goal is what one wants at the *finish*."[100] At the end is a new beginning: "Genet's generosity broadens out; he grows interested in other causes, he tries to help other men."[101] He cannot yet live the world that is his possibility because this world is not yet; but he knows this world is possible because he is living his future for the first time as its possibility.

Genet's case is meant to be exemplary, as are all psychoanalytic cases. It carries the message that we must give up the limitlessness of the imaginary that cripples us as beings by alienating us from what is real about ourselves and the world that is the foundation of our possibilities. We are fragile beings and will always be haunted by the terrifying dangers of non-being. Did not Freud state this clearly in "Civilization and Its Discontents"? What he did not state, leaving us in a state of confusion, is that we have confused the scarcity of things in the world which we need to survive with a scarcity of being. Being is not scarce; it is a plenitude because it brings itself into being in a world in which there is a plenitude of other beings it needs as its foundation. It is a matter of discovering that we want what we need. This, in turn, is a matter of destroying the illusions that alienate us from wanting each other. Sartre ends Genet's beginning with the beginning of a "generosity". Genet is moving from the darkness that we all sink into that conceals from us our own desires that are there, constitutive of our being from the beginning. He discovers that to stand transparently before the other in open face-to-face exchanges is the only possibility any of us have for supporting the vulnerable fragility of the freedom that is our being. Can this condition of being a transparent vulnerability that surrenders itself to another while gesturing to another to surrender its vulnerability be called anything but love? Sartre supplies a vision of human possibility that completes psychoanalytic theory by defining the work of consciousness, which justifies that theory, as a work of liberating the self's primordial power to love from a terrible violence committed on it by the world. Love must be liberated, because it is love which discovers the other as the prop upon which the self's realization of its possibilities depends. The violence of the world has twisted love into passion on whose horizon the self knows the other as the object it needs but does not want. On the horizon of love the self discovers the other as the site on which need is fused with want, opening it to its possibilities.

The case of Flaubert is manifestly organized around the theme of love. Although by far more massive in size than Genet, structurally it is not radically different. The purpose is to know Flaubert completely. Although the method of analysis in Flaubert follows a somewhat more formalized application of the "progressive - regressive" method outlined in "Search for a Method", its logic remains grounded in the fundamentals of psychoanalysis: "Each piece of data" gleaned from Flaubert's life, including his writings, "set in its place becomes a portion of the whole, which is constantly being created, and by the same token reveals its profound homogeneity with all other parts that make up the whole".[102]

The starting point that sets Flaubert's life into motion as a struggle with himself is the same as in Genet: what Flaubert himself referred to as "the deep, always hidden wound".[103] In Flaubert, Sartre names the wound the absence of love. It is not a spiritual or psychic wound which begins Flaubert's life, but a wound dealt to the body named as the original site which originates the desire for love. In Flaubert, the beginning is named as the body not the word. This actually positions Sartre both closer to and more distant from Freud than he is in "Being and Nothingness." He is closer because he does not read Freud across the Cartesian distance in which the subject's own body is known to him as if it were outside him in the world as a reference point for the self. In "Being and Nothingness" consciousness exhausts knowledge of itself when it knows itself as a transcendent surpassing toward the meaning of the physicality of the world, including the physical body. The body, known as if it were an Other that is part of the world, poses the same danger to freedom as does the world: the danger of falling into the horror of the pure physicality of sensation to be lost forever as a transcendent consciousness. In Flaubert the body is an animated intentional body which informs the intentionality of consciousness toward the meaning of the world. The boundaries of the self enclose the body in the kind of intimate relationship we are used to contemplating in Freud. Sartre, however, also distances himself from Freud by presenting the animated intentional body in this relationship as innocent of being the original site of the self's struggle with itself. The body, in the beginning, is an innocent need for attachment to another. Flaubert is innocent in the beginning, but it is not the passive innocence of Genet about to be separated from an illusion of attachment by a dramatic blow that leaves him with the experience of being exiled without cause. It is rather the innocence of someone who, needing an attachment to others is actively prepared to earn it. In brief, Flaubert is innocent because he is a normal child, who "when, bewildered and still 'brutish'... emerges from infancy" to find that "skills await him. And roles. Training begins".[104] Flaubert, like all children, begins as a little alien animal prepared to become human, but it is up to the rest of us to help make him so. What awaits Flaubert is his fall, because, as Sartre tells us, there has never yet been a child attached to the world without a wounding fall, since that is possible only in a world we have not yet made. Everything attests to Flaubert's fall beginning at the moment when training begins, especially Flaubert's encounter with language which, for all children, marks the end of infancy. Flaubert, "this future writer stumbled when it came to the prime test, his apprenticeship in words... he made a poor showing in the... chief initiation and rite of passage - learning the alphabet".[105] Sartre notes that "we are told that the child cried bitterly, that he was avid for knowledge, and that his impotence made him miserable." We are also shown something else, however. "We are shown a blustering dunce, stubborn in his refusal to learn... The second attitude implies a *combative relationship* between the child and his parents..."[106] Language is the medium of combat by which the family intitiates the violence that produces the family idiot. Language itself is like an innocent party in this combat. Indeed, it is not too much to say that in Sartre, language is the only innocence we can find so far in human history and as such is our hope. Freud, on the other hand, inventor of the technique for revealing what language conceals, has almost nothing to say about language as hope. Language represents the intentions of instinctual forces and energies which always produce a language of deceptive double meanings. Hope in Freud lies elsewhere than in the hope of ever speaking a language sanitized of its duplicity.

This duplicity is at the core of the child Gustave's stubborn combative idiocy. For Sartre, language is both the raw material out of which a child forms a knowledge of himself by being first known by others, and the raw material out of which freedom makes something more of itself than has been given. No wonder, Sartre tells us, the child first approaches language with a naive faith: no wonder little Gustave "cannot imagine that adults would deceive through caprice. After all, Descartes finds no other guarantee of human knowledge: God is good, therefore he has no desire to deceive us. A valid reason. For Gustave, it is more than a reason, it is a basic right".[107] This is a right history has yet to honor for any of us. "All parents are jokers; fooled since childhood themselves, they take pleasure in fooling their own youngsters, out of kindness. It never occurs to them that they might be driving their children crazy. The little victims must make do with the false feelings attributed to them, which they internalize, and with the false information that will be denied a moment later or soon afterward. These triflings are not always criminal; the child grows up, frees himself through questioning and refusal, coldly observes grownups fooling children. Yet Gustave remains marked". [108]

However deceitful it may be, the child Flaubert can no more resist language than can any child. What Gustave can and does resist is the comprehension of language. "An idea that is comprehended is me, and it is all that is not-me - it is *my* subjectivity exploding and collapsing, leaving my essence to be absorbed by the object. But am I ever freer and more unconditionally myself than in this 'perpetual combustion' that continually expands until it embraces everything? In the same way, language is *me* and *I* am language...And in the spiral garland of words must be seen, too, *myself in the Other*".[109] What Gustave resists, by treating language "as if - in the sense that we talk of stones singing and fountains weeping - language were... only noise speaking"[110], is the combustible play of freedom seeing others in itself and itself in others. That is to say, what Gustave resists is putting the intentionality of his subjectivity into active play in a world of active intentions carried by the activity of language. It is not Gustave's fault, Sartre hastens to assure us. "If Gustave, aged six, confuses sign and meaning to the extent that the material presence of the sign is the evidence that guarantees the truth of the meaning, he must have had a poor initial relationship with the Other".[111] In other words, if we are to understand what looks from the outside like the perfect passivity of Gustave's infancy before he is presented with the opportunity to be trained in decoding signs, we must understand where this passivity fits into the unity of an original project. The idea of an "original project" in Flaubert is far different from Baudelaire's original choice of himself. Nevertheless, the psychoanalytic eye must still see beneath the passivity to the seething activity that makes passivity possible.

In Flaubert, Sartre, relegating psychoanalysis to an auxiliary discipline specializing in human development, has made a peace of sorts with psychoanalytic language. He is comfortable in using the psychoanalytic language of conflict and defense to describe Flaubert's original project. The idea of a "project" is now reduced to the "brutish" not yet human infant and child pursuing what he needs that will lift him to his human possibilities. Conflict is the wound caused by the Other depriving the infant and child of what he needs. Defense is the response to the violence of that deprivation, which becomes the twisted version of the original project. Gustave's defense follows the formula Sartre uses in Genet and his own case: a subject consigned to exile from the possibilities of the world pursues a project of reversing the order of mirror and image imposed on him by the violence of the world. Defense is a subject's desperate pursuit of a way out of the conflict, like an animal caught in a trap repeatedly chewing on its leg to find a way to cure its wound.

Sartre reads Gustave's particular defense disclosed in a particular story, *Quidquid volueris*, which Gustave wrote at the age of fifteen. The story concerns an ape man Djalioh, produced by a scientist in the interests of science, out of the rape of a female slave by an orangutan. "It is clear that Djalioh, the apeman, represents Flaubert himself... That is, Djalioh is *arrested in childhood*, just beyond the point at which man and animal are - according to Gustave - still indistinguishable".[112] Djalioh is Gustave, escaping through the imaginary, the agonizing trap of his human identity as exile. Djalioh, the non-human, is Gustave standing alone as the sole occupant of a non-human world, the imaginary avenger, we might say, who has reversed the order of mirror and image imposed on him by the violence of his birth. "At fifteen" Sartre observes, "Gustave assigns to the birth of Djalioh the function Pascal assigns to the Fall: that of an absolute beginning. Neither angel nor beast, says Pascal... And Flaubert, neither beast nor man. By his origin, in effect, Djalioh, the son of a woman, escapes the *general essence* which characterizes orangutans; the son of an ape, he escapes what the young author believes to be *human* nature".[113] It is something like the ultimate escape Freud sees driving the unconscious into the paternal bond: the exhorbitant limitless fantasy of becoming the father of oneself. At the same time, the story Gustave wrote is part of his struggle with himself to transcend his arrested childhood in a movement toward the possibilities of the world. "At fifteen the young boy has passed... from flexible defense to counterattack. He begins by accepting the judgment of other people, by pushing it to an extreme... and hurls the accusation back on his accusers. Ape-man - why not? Be animals if you can, strictly subhuman, anything rather than human beings".[114] It is the old game of loser-wins. The game is the defensive project which Flaubert is to play as his life. Like Genet's game, it is also repeated as a struggle in his life to transcend the limitless fantasies that fuel it toward the end which set it in motion: the discovery of the self as freedom at play within the limits of a world supported by a love that is freedom's possibility.

Aptly enough, Sartre sees both the wounding and the project disclosed in an archetypal scene centering on the paternal bond. "As [Gustave] runs, smiling, to throw himself into his father's open arms, he is consciously determined by a sign that embodies a signified relationship between lord and vassal. Better, it is a *sign* rather than a caress. Why does he crave it if not because it *signifies* paternal love?".[115] Gustave's original project, born not out of his choice but imposed on him by his normalcy as a human child is given the name only alluded to in Genet: the pursuit of love. Yet the cause of Gustave's wound does not lie in the bad luck of having a depriving father, it lies rather in a step earlier on the developmental ladder, the infant's relations to his mother. But that is not the real cause either. Sartre sees the real cause where Freud always seemed to miss it in his cases starting with Dora. The cause lies in the history of Gustave's time, which like our time, causes Gustave, like all of us, to be "a bad fit in the linguistic universe, that is in the social order, *in the family*".[116] The first relations of infant to mother bear the terrible burden of that bad fit.

"Where do the troubles begin, the aversions and the impossibilities?".[117] Sartre's answer to his question points to the infant's relationship to its mother, so often bemoaned by Freud's revisionists as totally neglected by him. What they mean is that the mother appears too late in Freud's work, as part of the Oedipal triangle. It is necessary for her to appear at the very beginning of the life of the infant in order to anchor the end of the story of development, as a story which leaves conflict and defense behind, to a beginning that already contains the end. What was impossible in Baudelaire, Sartre assumes in Flaubert: the role of developmental psychoanalyst. Sartre provides the essentials: "The distinctive features of the six-year-old child [Gustave]... can be reduced to two basic determinations: one is the pathic character of his sensibility, the other is a certain 'difficulty of being' which translates as a certain psychosomatic unease. If these tendencies were formed in the course of his prehistory, they must indicate a problem in the original relationship that binds the child, flesh in the process of blossoming, to the progenetrix, woman making herself flesh in order to nourish, nurture, and caress the flesh of her flesh".[118] The mother, through physically caring for her infant "achieves a relationship... which can be called maternal love".[119] Consistent with contemporary developmental theory, Sartre insists that he is referring to maternal love as "a relationship and not a feeling".[120] It is the original relationshp with the mother that the infant "internalizes... as the passivity which conditions all the drives and inner appetite rhythms, promptings and accumulated storms, schemes revealing at once organic constants and inexpressible desires - briefly, his own mother, absorbed into his body's innermost depths, becomes the pathic structure of his affective nature".[121]

It is Caroline, Gustave's mother who deals him his original hidden wound - or rather, if we are to be true to Sartre's description of their original relationship, Caroline *is* the wound Gustave has no choice but to take into himself. It is not Caroline's fault that she herself emerged as a wound from her family. The reproduction of family wounds is how capitalist societies reproduce themselves. Sartre's speculations on Caroline's origins can be summed up by saying that her wounds led her, orphaned as a young girl, into a marriage with Achille-Cleophas Flaubert, a physician, to found a family marked by the bourgeois tensions of the mid-nineteenth century. They wanted children who, like possessions, would insure their immortality. Gustave's father wanted boys, of course, but Caroline, secretly tortured by her own orphaning as a child, wanted a daughter. The first was a boy, Achille, who belonged to her husband. Family planning demanded more children as insurance. Two dead sons followed, and then Gustave. "Poor Caroline, she must have hoped and despaired, sometimes welcoming a future daughter as celestial manna, at other times spitting into the ashes to deny the imminent son... After which the midwife delivered her of a boy... If my hypothesis is accurate," states Sartre, "the young mother viewed him as an alien creature; she had too fervently hoped to reproduce herself - in the literal sense of the word - not to resent the fact that an interloper had been created without permission in the flesh of her flesh. An Other".[122]

More insurance, and Caroline finally has her daughter, the new Caroline. In the meantime, she does her duty, as a good bourgeois wife and mother and takes care of Gustave. There is no question of love in her touch and her caress. She had loved her dead sons as she loved Gustave: "With a general love which... respected the sex of the father in them and the future glory of the Flauberts".[123] It is not Caroline's fault; it is how patriarchal cultures all reproduce themselves, in one way or another, and in different ways for the different sexes - by twisting love into a wounding instrument inside the body of the infant. It is as if Sartre were saying that in a society where wounds are plentiful and cures scarce, every sex must be the wrong sex for somebody. As for the beginning of Gustave's story, "this is a fabrication, I confess" Sartre tells us[124] "I have no proof that it was so... Never mind... I can imagine without the least vexation... precisely the contrary of what I invent, but *in any case* it will have to follow the paths I have indicated and refute my explanation on the ground I have determined - the body and love".[125] In other words, we are invited to read the psychoanalytic case - this fiction that is not a fiction, which is to say, a psychoanalytic *interpretation* of a life - and by following its psychoanalytic logic, confront not the facts of Flaubert's origin, which nobody can ever know in any case, but the truth of our own projects. Can anyone ever read a psychoanalytic case with any other end in mind than that of finding in its interpretations of another's struggles interpretations of his own struggles which allow him to begin to understand himself better?

The ends we pursue must have a beginning that contains the end if they are to be coherent. Flaubert is meant to exemplify all our beginnings. "And what about [Gustaves's] malaise? This is not a matter of conjecture: a child must have a *mandate to live*, the parents are the authorities who issue the mandate. A grant of love..."[126] The absence of a mandate of love at the beginning is a wound of alienation that starts a life separated from the experience of living its purposes as its own. The beginning is everything. With a mandate of love at the beginning a child will be able to experience a purpose to his life as its very fabric. The parental mandate of love reveals to Gustave the direction in which his life must move. In other words, the road to a subject's realization of his possibilities is the realization of the ability to love; and this ability must come to him first from the outside, delivered to him in the beginning by love.

In a very real sense, all three thousand pages of "A Family Idiot" is Sartre's paean to love. Once unthinkable to him, it ends with a flourish that was also once unthinkable, but is like an elaboration of the theoretical mistake Binswanger told Freud he was making: the mistake of not valorizing the religious impulse. "If he has truly received the fullness of early parental attentions consecrated by the scattered smiles of the world" Sartre says of all human beings, "if he has found absolute sovereignty in the earliest part of his life, before weaning, things will go even farther. The supreme end will accept becoming the unique means of fulfilling those who adore him and for whom he is the reason for being; living will be the *passion* - in the religious sense - that will transform self-centeredness into a gift; experience will be felt as *the free exercise of generosity*".[127] Religion, like opium, induces visions, and visions are a two-edged sword; they can cut us off from the world, or they can open up the world. In this sense, Sartre is reading, like other acolytes, Marx's essential message.

Without the mandate of love, we all carry into the history of our lives, to one extent or another and in one way or another, Gustave's original experience of alienation: "Gustave is the victim of a mystification; since nothing is expected of him as the singular subject of his history, he will therefore be its object. Without a particular mission he is deprived, *from the start*, of the cardinal categories of praxis. Not that the future entirely escapes his purview, but... he sees it as the ineluctable result of an alien will; it can be prophesied but not *shaped*, since it is already accomplished".[128] We have covered barely two percent of "The Family Idiot", nevertheless Sartre has already welded together concepts from ontology, psychoanalytic psychology, and Marxist socio-economic history into a frame on which to hang the coherency of the story of Flaubert's life. As Gustave becomes Flaubert he cannot avoid struggling with the very defenses he develops to escape the conflict that posseses him. This struggle is the forward movement of his life. It is only a question of following the torques, reversals, twists, hesitations and doubts that constitute for him, as they did for Genet, the cunning but unconscious rules for playing and replaying the game of "loser-wins". It is also a question of following the progress of this play and replay toward its appointed end. Flaubert's life moves from desperate attempts to escape into the Imaginary where in "the deepest solitude, the solitude *of the beast*"[129] he imagines he possesses himself totally, to where he "will define himself by *desire*, that is, sumptuously and universally by everything he does not have".[130] Like the Parisian students at the barricades in 1968 whom Sartre admired, Flaubert, living as passion wants what passion wants: everything. His desires are infinite, but *"it is the essence of infinite desire to desire the impossible. Or, if you like, self conscious impossibility awakens desire and exalts it; impossibility endows it with its rigor and its violence, and desire rediscovers impossibility outside in the object as the fundamental category of the desirable"*.[131] Useless passions, once identified by Sartre as the definition of a human life like Baudelaire's which has no place to go, are now a phase, a stage, an historical moment in a story about a human life which is going somewhere. We cannot expect Flaubert to make it to the end. No one can alone, not even Sartre. For Sartre, it takes a revolutionary enterprise, in the socio-political sense, to create culture as a space in which freedom can live its experience of itself as freedom.

Sartre knows, of course, that revolution is fueled by the violence of passion. In the dreams of every revolutionary for a different life violence is necessary if it is to be left behind. But we would miss the point of the movement of Sartre's work into the revisionist scene of reading Freud if we saw only this as its point, as so many readers of Sartre are prone to do. What links Sartre to the revisionist scene of reading Freud is not the issue of the necessity of revolutionary violence, but the dream which every psychoanalyst, revolutionary or not, dreams in the scene of his patient's transference: that his patient's violent dreams of passion can be left behind. Sartre, in effect, presents us with Flaubert, the universal patient of our historical time, infected with the terrible malady of alienation, as if he were presenting the dream that psychoanalytic revisionists have for their patients' cure: discovering themselves by emerging from the violent fantasies that govern their lives. Flaubert discovers himself by emerging from his fantasies into the lived experience of the Real which points to the space of the world as his possibility. This discovery is the end of the beginning and the beginning of the end.

True to the revisionist scene of reading Freud, passion, for Sartre, is not love. Passion fuels a work of consciousness that liberates love to be the "perpetual combustion"[132] of subjectivity which explodes into others and then collapses as others explode inside it. The discovery of love is the discovery of an adventure with others which is the sign that the self has discovered itself as the subject of its own possibilities. In Flaubert's case study, Sartre states clearly what he could not find in his own ontology of freedom presented in "Being and Nothingness" as the mystery of a pure spontaneity of choice, unsupported by anything, like a wisp of dark smoke, and which he could not find in the dark opacity of Freud's doctrine of instincts: liberating love is the work to which consciousness is called by a vision of possibility.

Sartre's ambition to change things, to turn possibility into the Real, carries him into the revisionist scene of reading Freud. There is room in the scene for the Sartres and the Eriksons, the Annas and the Binswangers. They share it on the basis of a common ambition: to make psychoanalysis live up to its promise to be part of The Great Human Project to change things by knowing everything, making everything opaque transparent, settling mysteries. Sartre is not the only child of Descartes. His ambition carries him into the revisionist scene of reading Freud because his ambition is incoherent unless it assumes that the world itself carries a mandate to love. Sartre must leave Baudelaire behind as the revisionist scene of reading Freud must leave Freud behind. Freud's failure lies precisely in failing to cohere psychoanalytic theory around a vision of possibility that carries the world's mandate to the self, defining its work of consciousness as a work of liberating love. The scene of reading Freud to complete him puts all of the themes of love at play in a space which casts no shadows on them as transparent truths - love as a primordial force within every human being that bonds it to a world it needs and wants, the world organized around values which give density to visions of possibility that command the mandate of love, and passion as the struggle between love and a violence inflicted on it which twists it into an endless nightmare of repeating the search for the impossible.

No one can find anything like this shadowless space in Freud. One can only find the space of the transference filled with the dark shadows of a passion that needs but does not want the world, which leads revisionists like Sartre, to read Freud from a scene that completes him with something, if not identical to Sartre's paean to love, then with something very much like it.

References

1 Jean-Paul Sartre, *Being and Nothingness*, tr. Hazel E. Barnes, New York, Washington Square Press, 1966, p. 590.

2 Ibid., p. 589

3 Ibid., p. 590

4 Ibid., p. 590

5 Ibid., p. 590

6 Ibid., p. 590

7 Ibid., p. 590

8 Ibid., p. 590-591

9 Dominick LaCapra, *A Preface to Sartre*, Ithaca, Cornell University Press, 1978, p. 29.

10 Ibid., p. 172.

11 Douglas Collins, *Sartre as Biographer*, Cambridge, Harvard University Press, 1980, p. 22.

12 Jean-Paul Sartre, *Saint Genet*, New York, New American Library, 1971, p. 17.

13 Jean-Paul Sartre, *The Family Idiot*, V. I, tr. Carol Cosman, Chicago, The University of Chicago Press, 1981, p. 132.

14 Michael Scriven, *Sartre's Existential Biographies*, New York, St. Martin's Press, 1984, p. 116 - 117.

15 Jean-Paul Sartre, The Family Idiot, V. I, 1981 p. x.

16 Jean-Paul Sartre, *Between Existentialism and Marxism*, tr. John Mathews, New York, Pantheon Books, 1974, p. 44-46.

17 Madeleine Chapsal, "'To Show, To Demonstrate...'", *Yale French Studies*, 30, [1963], p. 39.

18 Roy Schafer, *The Analytic Attitude*, New York, Basic Books, 1983, p. 113.

19 Ibid., p. 194.

20 Ibid., p. 194.

21 Ibid., p. 194.

22 Ibid., p. 196.

23 Ibid., p. 194.

24 Jean-Paul Sartre, *Baudelaire*, tr. Martin Turnell, New York, New Directions, 1950, p. 16.

25 Ibid., p. 192.

26 Maurice Merleau-Ponty, *Sense and Non-Sense*, tr. Hubert L. Dreyfus and Patricia Allen Dreyfus, Evanston, Northwestern University Press, 1964, p. 72.

27 Jean-Paul Sartre, Baudelaire, 1950, p. 16-17.

28 Ibid., p. 17.

29 Ibid., p. 17.

30 Jean-Paul Sartre, Being and Nothingness, 1966, p. 63.

31 Jean-Paul Sartre, Baudelaire, 1950, p. 19.

32 Ibid., p. 19.

33 Ibid., p. 20.

34 Jean-Paul Sartre, Being and Nothingness, 1966, p.618-619.

35 Ibid., p. 616

36 Ibid., p. 616

37 Ibid., p. 735

38 Jean-Paul Sartre, Baudelaire, 1950, p. 20.

39 Jean-Paul Sartre, Being and Nothingness, 1966, p. 738.

40 Ibid., p. 738

41 Jean-Paul Sartre, Baudelaire, 1950, p. 22.

42 Iris Murdoch, Sartre:Romantic Rationalist, 1953, p. 95.

43 Edward Erwin, "Psychoanalysis and Self-Deception" in Brian P. McLaughlin and Amelie Oksenberg Rorty eds., *Perspectives on Self-Deception*, Berkeley, University of California Press, 1988, p.240.

44 Leila Tov-Ruach, "Freud on Unconscious Affects, Mourning and the Erotic Mind", in McLaughlin and Rorty eds. 1988, p. 252.

45 Joseph P. Fell, *Emotion in the Thought of Sartre*, New York, Columbia University Press, 1965, p. vii.

46 Ibid., p. 13

47 Jean-Paul Sartre, *The Emotions*, tr. Bernard Frechtman, New York, Wisdom Library, 1948, p. 58-59.

48 Jean-Paul Sartre, Being and Nothingness, 1966, p. 39.

49 Herbert Fingarette, *Self-Deception*, New York, Humanities Press, 1969, p. 50.

50 Jean-Paul Sartre, Being and Nothingness, 1966, p. 100.

51 Jean-Paul Sartre, Baudelaire, 1950, p. 29-31.

52 Jean-Paul Sartre, Being and Nothingness, 1966, p. 43.

53 Ibid., p. 44.

54 Dominick LaCapra, A Preface to Sartre, 1978, p.175.

55 Jean-Paul Sartre, Baudelaire, 1950, p. 24.

56 Ibid., p. 91-92.

57 Jean-Paul Sartre, Being and Nothingness, 1966, p. 796.

58 Jean-Paul Sartre, Baudelaire, 1950, p. 116.

59 Dominick LaCapra, A Preface to Sartre, 1978, p. 26-27.

60 Jean-Paul Sartre, Being and Nothingness, 1966, p. 798.

61 Ibid., p. 765.

62 Ibid., p. 771.

63 Ibid., p. 777.

64 Ibid., p. 778.

65 Ibid., p. 303.

66 Ibid., p. 343-344.

67 R. D. Laing and D. G. Cooper, *Reason and Violence*, New York, Vintage Books, 1971, p. 68.

68 Ibid., p. 73.

69 Jean-Paul Sartre, Saint Genet, 1971, p. 35.

70 Jean-Paul Sartre, *Search for a Method*, tr. Hazel E. Barnes, New York, Vintage Books, 1963, p. 8.

71 Jean-Paul Sartre, *Critique of Dialectical Reason*, tr. Alan Sheridan-Smith, London, Verso/NLB, 1982, p. 80.

72 Ibid., p. 81.

73 Ibid., p. 81-82.

74 Ibid., p. 83.

75 Ibid., p. 90.

76 Ibid., p. 91.

77 Ibid., p. 123.

78 Ibid., p. 113.

79 Jean-Paul Sartre, Saint Genet, 1971, p. 1.

80 Ibid. p. 17.

81 Ibid., p. 2.

82 Ibid., p. 6.

83 Ibid., p. 7.

84 Ibid., p. 7.

85 Ibid., p. 6.

86 Ibid., p. 36.

87 Ibid., p. 36.

88 Ibid., p. 37.

89 Ibid., p. 49-50.

90 Jean-Paul Sartre, *The Words*, tr. Bernard Frechtman, New York, George Braziller, 1964, p. 160.

91 Ibid., p. 159.

92 Ibid., p. 158.

93 Jean-Paul Sartre, Saint Genet, 1971, p. 425.

94 Ibid., p. 449.

95 Ibid., p. 454.

96 Ibid., p. 544.

97 Ibid., p. 561.

98 Ibid., p. 570.

99 Jean-Paul Sartre, Baudelaire, 1950, p. 21.

100 Jean-Paul Sartre, Saint Genet, 1971, p. 582.

101 Ibid., p. 582.

102 Jean-Paul Sartre, The Family Idiot, V. 1, 1981, p. ix.

103 Ibid., p. x.

104 Ibid., p. 3.

105 Ibid., p. 3.

106 Ibid., p. 4.

107 Ibid., p. 10.

108 Ibid., p. 10.

109 Ibid., p. 12.

110 Ibid., p. 14.

111 Ibid., p. 14.

112 Ibid., p. 19.

113 Ibid., p. 20.

114 Ibid., p. 20.

115 Ibid., p. 18.

116 Ibid., p. 11.

117 Ibid., p. 18.

118 Ibid., p. 46-47.

119 Ibid., p. 47.

120 Ibid., p. 47.

121 Ibid., p. 47-48.

122 Ibid., p. 126.

123 Ibid., p. 127.

124 Ibid., p. 132.

125 Ibid., p. 132.

126 Ibid., p. 133.

127 Ibid., p. 133-134.

128 Ibid., p. 136.

129 Ibid., p. 626

130 Ibid., p. 411

131 Ibid., p. 413

132 Ibid., p. 12

Part 4

Freud's Last Word

Nowhere does Freud's work contest itself as in his sociocultural texts. These texts, including "Beyond the Pleasure Principle" and the "Ego and the Id", adumbrate rather than state forthrightly the warning about love that is Freud's cohering last word. Freud, no stranger to being a scandal, was also no stranger to the anxiety of being a scandalizer who presents psychoanalysis as a suspicion of love to a world which never tires of singing paeans to love, albeit, as often as not, with a bad conscience. While Freud never calls consciousness to any other work than that of suspicion, this work receives its final definition from a warning about love delivered in a typically guarded way at the end of "Group Psychology and the Analysis of the Ego": We must read in the scenes of history the dangers of love as a force, which, able to dissolve the boundary between superego and ego, beloved and lover, leader and follower, is the sign of the death instinct asserting dominion over Eros.

"The Ego and the Id" sets the stage. Freud, reducing the self to the status of a meaning-effect of the instinctual conflict between Eros and the death instinct, presents us with a play within a play: the mind as the structure of life is troped as a drama played out on the stage of the world as history. In "The Ego and the Id", the concept of ego, a shadowy figure in all of Freud's previous texts rarely designating simply the individual, is brought stage center and presented as "one of the protagonists in the conflict splitting the individual"[1] that links the two dramas. Ego includes consciousness, but is not identical to consciousness. It is responsible for repression, but the unconscious itself "does not coincide with what is repressed...A part of the ego too - and Heaven knows how important a part - may be unconscious... and this unconscious belonging to the ego is not latent like the preconscious..."[2] In his famous anatomical diagram of the mind, Freud depicts the ego with clear boundaries that differentiate it from the external world. By contrast, "the ego is not sharply separated from the id; its lower portion merges into it".[3] As a result, we arrive at Freud's famous metaphor for ego's relations to the id: ego "is like a man on horseback who has to hold in check the superior strength of the horse; with this difference, that the rider seeks to do so with his own strength while the ego uses borrowed forces." Like a rider who finds himself in the awkward position of having to guide the horse where the horse wants to go, "the ego constantly carries into action the wishes of the id as if they were its own".[4] The metaphor is limited in one further respect. The id is not monolithic. The ego is not like a thirsty rider in a Western movie who can give the horse its rein, sensing that it will lead him to water. "Eros and the death instinct struggle within [the Id]..."[5] The Id, once referring in Freud's work to a force antagonistic to ego's accommodating the reality principle, is now the site of contesting forces.

Freud reviews it again for us: "The clamor of life proceeds for the most part from Eros. And from the struggle against Eros!".[6] Love binds the world together and provides the momentum for its history. But love cannot escape the claims of the death instinct, which is why love only takes the form of a repetition of passion, which Sartre brilliantly labels the game of loser-wins. Ego must honor the claims of the death instinct from the beginning, because both Eros and the death instinct constitute the content of the id. Ambivalence, the precondition for the sequence of identification and internalization which sets life into motion, is the sign of the invisible contest going on in the dark between the two instincts. Abstracted from the precondition which makes them possible, however, the sequence of identification and internalization can be thought of as the work of sublimation which fulfills the claims made by Eros on the ego. Ego, loving another it identifies as its ideal, and then carrying that ideal into itself by withdrawing libido from the object toward itself, is the precondition for sublimation. "When the ego assumes the features of the object, it forces itself, so to speak, upon the id as a love object and tries to make good the loss of that object by saying, 'Look, I am so like the object, you can as well love me'"[7] which would be to love both ego and object now fused into one. Moving libido from the object pole toward the narcissistic pole, is like ego staging itself to move on and seek new objects to love to fulfill the purpose of Eros which "aims at complicating life by bringing about a more and more far-reaching coalescence of the particles into which living matter has been dispersed; thus, of course, aiming at the maintenance of life."[8]

Ego, however, is not the ally of Eros, but a victim caught in an ironic trap. Since ego cannot escape honoring the claims of the death instinct, it must enact the irony of fulfilling with a single stroke two irreconcilable and conflicting claims on it, satisfying neither and thereby increasing the claims of each. The act of falling in love with an object, which is the same as idealizing it, and then withdrawing libido to internalize it, does not only represent Eros' command to fuse with all of the objects of the world until boundaries themselves that support desire disappear from the world. It also represents the command of the death instinct which seeks a shortcut to the same end. In other words, the sequence of identification and internalization, which pulls libido from the object to the narcissistic pole, is also ego's way of meeting the claims of the death instinct. The work of sublimation weakens Eros' hold on the libido. "By... obtaining possession of the libido from the object-cathexes, setting itself up as sole love object, and desexualizing or sublimating the libido of the id, the ego is working in opposition to the purposes of Eros and placing itself at the service of the opposing instinctual trends."[9] The aim of the death instinct is to reduce the tension between desire and object to absolute zero. "But the falling of the level is delayed and fresh tensions are introduced by the claims of Eros..."[10] At the same time, sublimation must pass through the sequence of identification and internalization so that the claims of the death instinct can be brought to bear on the ego. The sign of this is that ego does not bring onto the interior stage only another as an ideal into whose boundaries it melds its own, but an other whose differentiating boundaries identify it as ego's nemesis called "superego". "The superego is... not merely a deposit left by the earliest object choices of the id; it also represents an energetic reaction formation against those choices. Its relation to the ego is not exhausted by the precept: 'You *ought to be* such and such [like your father]'; it also comprises the prohibition: 'You *must not be* such and such [like your father]...'"[11] Love, as in the case of the "Wolf Man", is preserved in the world under the sign of castration. Its destiny, from the first, is to arise in the world as the possibility of the social bond propped up by the violence of power. In this way the Oedipus complex is repressed, but "the strength to do this was, so to speak, borrowed from the father, and this loan was an extraordinarily momentous act. The superego retains the character of the father..."[12] History leaves nothing behind; the original struggle with the father is preserved by preserving the love for him. The struggle between ego and superego stages and restages the original struggle in the external world as the illusion of history.

Ego's response to Eros' claims on it uses the death instinct against itself. It is however, only the first fall in their match. The ironic outcome is that ego exposes itself to the death instinct which is using Eros against itself. The claims of the death instinct on ego cannot be asserted directly because, as Freud points out, while the relationship between the ego and the superego is one of struggle, "towards the two classes of instincts the ego's attitude is not impartial".[13] Ego must meet both the claims of Eros and the death instinct, but it has an obligation to itself in doing so. Simply put, it must stay on the horse. It has the obligation to keep itself alive, but this obligation is not the preface to a new drama Freud is about to present featuring ego's combat with death for the sake of life. Freud is as far as he can get from Darwin and as near as he can come to him. You cannot explain life, you can only depict its origin in a way that tries to illuminate its development. Ego is simply the name for an agent in a psychic drama whose structure is the definition of life, the origin of which Freud has already depicted for us in the primal horde story. Ego's obligation is to stay alive, not promote life. As a result its life has yet another ironic twist: it must seek its life from the very figure created out of itself which has put it under "the risk of itself becoming the object of the death instincts and of perishing".[14]

Freud depicts the risk in terms of the disorder of melancholia. Melancholia is a suitable example, in one sense, because it is a disorder in which the patient seems to push himself toward the very death he fears through his own self- abasement and self-vilification. Melancholia provides Freud with the ability to instruct us that "the fear of death concerns an interplay between the ego and the super-ego... The fear of death in melancholia only admits of one explanation: that the ego gives itself up because it feels itself hated and persecuted by the super-ego, instead of loved. To the ego, therefore, living means the same as being loved - being loved by the superego, which here again appears as the representative of the id".[15] Death wins in melancholia when the ego, seeing itself "deserted by all the forces of protection... lets itself die".[16] Ego has failed to disarm the cruelty of the superego by winning its love. How else can a rider who knows without knowing why that to live is to be loved, stay alive in desperate times trying to fulfill without knowing why, the obligation he did not choose of riding a horse which actually rides him, except by getting the horse to love him? These are the makings of a dire warning about love.

Toward the end of "The Ego and the Id", Freud again shows hesitation over speaking his own last word. Turning to melancholia, Freud is the clinician intercepting the momentum in his own theory toward presenting the sign of the death instinct's dominion over Eros in terms of the scenes of history where ego's struggle with the superego carries a warning about love. In melancholia ego dies from an absence of love and the scandal of love becomes not love but its absence. The innocence of love becomes validated as the question of defining a work of consciousness gravitates toward the question whose answer in Freud, always presumes the clinical encounter: how do we define the missing love that is the last word leading the patient to his possibility in the world? At the same time, in summing up the "Ego and the Id", Freud intimates that the superego's tormenting persecution of the ego does not exhaust the superego's strategies for leading ego to its death. "We have seen with what weapons the one group of instincts defends itself against the other",[17] or, adding what Freud leaves unspoken, asserts itself against the other. There must always be more to any picture of the ego's struggle with the superego than can meet the eye since the source of their struggle lies in an impenetrable darkness. Freud, in the "Ego and the Id", again refers us to the unknown as the last word. "It would be possible to picture the id as under the domination of the mute but powerful death instincts, which desire to be at peace and (as prompted by the pleasure principle) to put Eros, the mischief maker to rest; but perhaps that might be to undervalue the part played by Eros".[18]

Can we ever see everything? The struggle between ego and the superego is a struggle staged by cunning forces. The struggle for power proceeds through cunning, precisely as Freud taught us to see it staged in the transference, more than through naked force confronting naked force. Freud, inserting himself into the discourse on power, lays on the table the scandalous issue this century would rather avoid. The cunning weapon used by the superego in asserting the claims of the death instinct over an ego for whom to live is to be loved, is love itself. Darkness illuminates, and what it illuminates are the scenes of history in which the cunning death instinct struggles to use Eros against itself, making love the weapon for the death of life. It is a warning about love for which Freud lays the foundation in "The Ego and the Id", and speaks in "Group Psychology and the Analysis of the Ego". But the movement from one to the other passes through "Civilization and Its Discontents".

There is nothing much that is theoretically new in "Civilization and Its Discontents". Freud is clearing the decks for a redefinition of the work of consciousness in terms of a warning about love by systematically destroying philosophies of life that offer themselves as visions of possibility to be loved. What kind of vision of possibility can arise from the appeal which ends the book to "the other of the two 'Heavenly Powers' eternal Eros" to "make an effort to assert himself in the struggle with his equally immortal adversary." And from the final sentence appended a year after the book was published: "But who can foresee with what success and with what result?"[19] All that can arise from these last words, because the justification of psychoanalysis demands it, is a call to a work of consciousness to add whatever counterweight it can to the instinctual struggle going on in the dark to keep life going.

Freud begins by inserting psychoanalysis into the apparently interminable debate over whether there is a purpose to life. As we might expect he takes the negative side, directing his attack toward religion. It is not, however, quite the same attack he launched in "The Future of an Illusion" on the basis of psychoanalysis representing the scientific virtue of dealing with the how of things rather than the why of them. His opening theme is a preamble to the new attack: "It is impossible to escape the impression that people commonly use false standards of measurement - that they seek power, success and wealth for themselves and admire them in others, and that they underestimate what is of true value in life. And yet, in making any general judgment of this sort, we are in danger of forgetting how variegated the human world and its mental life are".[20] His friend Romain Rolland has reminded him that there is a single feeling that underlies orthodox religions which call us to life's purpose - the commonplace feeling that we are part of "something limitless, unbounded, - as it were, 'oceanic',", which is the source of the human religious impulse.[21] "One may... rightly call oneself religious on the ground of this oceanic feeling alone, even if one rejects every belief and every illusion."[22] Freud sees clearly that what is at stake for Rolland is the power of love to cure us of being estranged from the world as a self that is "autonomous and unitary, marked off distinctly from everything else".[23] He addresses the issue forthrightly. Love does indeed give us the feeling that "the boundary between ego and object threatens to melt away",[24] but this is no reason to embrace religious visions. On the contrary, the experience, and the religious impulse it expresses, are no more than a residual trace of the original limitless demands of the pleasure principle against the reality principle which rules our relations to the world.

Freud's reply to Rolland has the thrust of humbling the pride love takes in declaring itself a revelation about the purpose of life. Its net effect is to appropriate the terms of the debate, shifting it onto his ground. Religion may claim it knows love, but it is psychoanalysis which knows it, and knows it as pursuing the purposes of the pleasure principle. Psychoanalysis, in effect, reveals that the purpose of human life is given to life at the moment life exists as body. "What decides the purpose of life is simply the programme of the pleasure principle. This principle dominates the operation of the mental apparatus from the start."[25] The question of the purpose of life is not quite made senseless by this, but the debate is now shifted to the question of whether there are values that humans can love which can command the movement of history toward realizing culture as the site on which the possibilities of happiness can be fulfilled. "There can be no doubt about the pleasure principle's efficacy, and yet its programme is at loggerheads with the whole world, with the macrocosm as well as the microcosm".[26] Nevertheless, it is possible to debate whether any of those "commanding images", as Nisbet puts it, which humans use to envision the movement of history as "growth and development in civilizations and societies and cultures" as "a kind of unfolding of internal potentiality, the whole moving toward some end that is presumably contained in the process from the start",[27] have any validity in defining human expectations for at least a reasonable measure of happiness.

Freud takes us through the possibilities with the outcome determined in advance. Nothing can cure the split within us, transcending the pull of the primitive pleasure principle on the reality principle, or even allow a truce between the two principles in their contest to rule us. What it comes down to in the end, is that "it is impossible to overlook the extent to which civilization is built up upon a renunciation of instinct, how much it presupposes precisely the non-satisfaction (by suppression, repression, or some other means?) of powerful instincts. This 'cultural frustration' dominates the large field of social relationships between human beings".[28] Freud, however, is not preparing us for a stoical philosophy of endurance because culture is everywhere founded on a prescriptive and proscriptive Law which demands instinctual renunciation in order to deliver the benefits of order in human relationships. He insists, rather, that the problem of order must be reformulated as a problem and not a benefit. If we recognize "love as one of the foundations of civilization..." whose "power ... made the man unwilling to be deprived of his sexual object - the woman -, and made the woman unwilling to be deprived of the part of herself which had been separated off from her - her child",[29] then we must recognize that order should serve the function of love. But it does not. It is not "easy to understand how this civilization..." whose parents are "Eros and Ananke [Love and Necessity]... could act upon its participants otherwise than to make them happy".[30]

He is implicitly raising the issue of redefining Ananke in a way that cuts the ground from under a debate over a philosophy of life once and for all. It is clear that Eros, which rules the world, does not rule it alone. Yet what is Ananke? It must refer us to something different than environmental pressures that demand adaptation in the name of survival. It must be identified by understanding what it is that love wants. Rolland is right about the dream of love, but wrong about its meaning. He is right in implying that Eros dreams not of making history but of ending it. What he does not see in this dream, as does Freud, is that it is the ominous dream of passion to drain the horror from the movement of history by draining the horror of struggling with time from movement itself. Cathy and Heathcliff roaming the moors together for eternity.

Rolland cannot see passion in the dreams of love because all he can see in them is Eros. He does not see that ambivalence, from the beginning pervades love. He shrewdly senses Freud's own ambivalence about love, but he locates that ambivalence, as he does all ambivalence, in a narrative about the errors and mistakes made by an occluded consciousness that cannot discover love's possibilities. Rolland is following an old story, perhaps the oldest story that humans tell over and over again about their suffering in new and emotionally compelling versions. What else are visions of possibility that we proclaim we love but stories about getting history right once and for all - turning things rightside up so that as Marx put it, "the production of ideas, of conceptions, of consciousness, is above all directly interwoven into the material activity and the material interaction of people - and as such is the language of real life".[31] Living a fusion of language and reality is the end of the dream of ending history. Marx's dream is Capital's dream. The contest between them is only an illusion which misses the point.

"We need the same stories over and over," Miller tells us, "as one of the most powerful, perhaps *the* most powerful, of ways to assert the basic ideology of our culture." And then he asks and proceeds to answer the question: "Why do we always need more stories?...Because in some ways they do not satisfy. Stories, however perfectly conceived and powerfully written, however moving, do not accomplish successfully their allocated function."[32] But in Freud, we would have to say they do. Their function lies precisely in their repetition which is the movement of history that is precisely the story of human life in the form of passion striving to repeat itself in order not to go anywhere, in order not to reach its end.

The redefinition of Ananke that began in "Beyond the Pleasure Principle" is completed in "Civilization and Its Discontents". The entire movement of history must be recast into the necessity of the movement of passion whose end is to preserve a movement which goes nowhere - whose end, in effect, is to keep moving. Freud states it baldly enough in terms of the dual instincts thematized in "Beyond the Pleasure Principle": "The meaning of the evolution of civilization is no longer obscure to us. It must present the struggle between Eros and Death, between the instinct of life and the instinct of destruction, as it works itself out in the human species. This struggle is what all life essentially consists of, and the evolution of civilization may therefore be simply described as the struggle for life of the human species".[33] We can now see, in "Civilization and Its Discontents" the full significance of reversing the relationship between love and resistance. Resistance, the compulsion to repeat, is not the sign of the subject's struggle to realize the power of his love; it is the sign of the struggle for life. Darkness illuminates the stage of the world on which history is at play. "Civilization and Its Discontents" shows it illuminates it in terms of a distinction first proposed by Lagache: "We do not repeat our needs, we need to repeat."[34] If order preserves the world, then order is the compulsion to repeat, which takes the form of passion whose compulsion to repeat itself preserves the world because it goes nowhere even while dreaming other dreams.

The death instinct haunts culture, exerting a kind of gravitational pull on passion's compulsion to repeat itself to bring itself to an end, to a final solution.

No one escapes either the cycle of identification, rebellion, murder and reparation that is the foundation of the social bond whose sign is guilt, or the threat of the return of the repressed. In "Civilization and Its Discontents" Freud states precisely this as the problem of instinctual renunciation: If "originally renunciation of instinct was the result of fear of an external authority", that is, if "one renounced one's satisfactions in order not to lose its love", then, "if one has carried out this renunciation, one is, as it were, quits with the authority and no sense of guilt should remain".[35] But you can't escape the arm of the Law. Guilt arises "when the authority is internalized through the establishment of a super-ego".[36] If you can't get away from the Law, neither can you expect to get justice from it: "Instinctual renunciation now no longer has a completely liberating effect; virtuous continence is no longer rewarded with the assurance of love. A threatened external unhappiness - loss of love and punishment on the part of the external authority - has been exchanged for a permanent internal unhappiness, for the tension of the sense of guilt".[37] The assumption, that "first comes renunciation of instinct owing to fear of aggression by the *external* authority", simply will not do.[38] We must entertain instead the distinctly psychoanalytic idea that lies at the foundation of the scene of the primal horde. Renunciation is imposed not simply by the encounter of libidinal instincts with an external authority that forbids their pleasure, although this is certainly a critical component of the scene, but by aggressive instincts coupled to the libidinal instincts which makes "the renunciation in question ... always a renunciation of aggression".[39] If the possibility of the social bond depends on the erection of a superego in relation to which the subject loses himself in a violent drama of mirrors and masks - "If I were the father and you were the child, I should treat you badly" -[40] it is because "the original severity of the superego does not - or does not so much - represent the severity which one has experienced from ....[the authority object], or which one attributes to it; it represents, rather one's own aggressiveness towards it".[41]

Whatever equivocations Freud goes on to express about this view do not deter him from unequivocally stating: "Now, I think, we can at last grasp two things perfectly clearly: the part played by love in the origin of conscience and the fatal inevitability in the sense of guilt. Whether one has killed one's father or has abstained from doing so is not really the decisive thing. One is bound to feel guilty in either case, for the sense of guilt is the expression of the conflict due to ambivalence, of the eternal struggle between Eros and the instinct of destruction or death".[42]

In "Civilization and Its Discontents" Freud sees irony operating in the spectacle of the movement of history propelled by the play between violence and sublime visions of possibility. He also understands irony in terms of Allen Tate's characterization of it as that "which permits to the spectator an insight superior to that of the actor".[43] Irony is illumination that always comes from the dark. The decks are clear for a renewed look at the social bond in "Group Psychology and the Analysis of the Ego" that will convey his warning about love.

*

"Group Psychology and the Analysis of the Ego" is a book of warnings. Its set piece is Freud's opening discourse with Le Bon's classic warning about "rapidly formed and transient groups from which Le Bon has made his brilliant psychological character sketch of the group mind". Le Bon is warning us about groups, like crowds and mobs, in which "the particular acquirements of individuals become obliterated..."[44] The questions Freud wishes to address reverberate with the politically ominous language attributed to groups by Le Bon. "What... is a 'group'?" Freud asks, "How does it acquire the capacity for exercising such a decisive influence over the mental life of the individual? And what is the nature of the mental change which it forces upon the individual?"[45] Groups may be like instruments by which humans realize their desires in the world, but it is their dark side which makes both Le Bon and Freud anxious.

Freud ties himself to Le Bon's analysis of groups in which individual will is submerged by three strands. First, Le Bon's analysis is based on a psychology of regression. Freud quotes Le Bon favorably in this regard: "The individual forming part of a group acquires, solely from numerical considerations, a sentiment of invincible power which allows him to yield to instincts which, had he been alone, he would perforce have kept under constraint".[46] Second, Le Bon sees in the loss of individual will which characterizes his groups a parallel to the phenomenon of hypnotic influence from which Freud himself began his journey into psychoanalytic theory. He again quotes Le Bon favorably:

> An individual may be brought into such a condition that, having lost his conscious personality, he obeys all the suggestions of the operator who has deprived him of it, and commits acts in utter contradiction with his character and habits. The most careful investigations seem to prove that an individual immersed for some length of time in a group in action soon finds himself - either in consequence of the magnetic influence given out by the group, or from some other cause of which we are ignorant - in a special state of fascination in which the hypnotised individual finds himself in the hands of the hypnotiser... The conscious personality has entirely vanished; will and discernment are lost. All feelings and thoughts are bent in the direction determined by the hypnotiser.[47]

Finally, Le Bon's focusing on the similarity between his groups and individuals under the influence of hypnotic suggestion opens the door to bringing to bear on the problem of suggestibility that which belongs to psychoanalysis and no other discipline: love. "A group" Freud states, "is clearly held together by a power of some kind; and to what power could this feat be better ascribed than to Eros, who holds together everything in the world?"[48]

Freud, of course, by explaining that it is love which forms the bond in Le Bon's groups, intends to make Le Bon's warning into a psychoanalytic warning. Le Bon's groups, which are capable of acting like an undifferentiated mass without reason, can be understood only in the context of answering in psychoanalytic terms what makes the social bond itself possible. The answer must feature what Le Bon could not, the transference, relegating Le Bon's analysis to description rather than explanation.

The story Freud tells about the possibility of the social bond is not new. First, Freud will take us once again through the well known story of the Oedipus complex and its critical outcome, identification with the father. Identification with the father is possible because a feeling of love for him "is ambivalent from the very first; it can turn into an expression of tenderness as easily as into a wish for someone's removal".[49] Identification with the father as a love object leads to internalization of the father. The ego ideal is formed out of a narcissistic movement of libido from object to ego. It is only a short step from this to the possibility of the social bond exemplified by the group. This step is made apparent by the phenomenon of being in love, whose model for Freud, is always found in the scene of the transference. "In connection with this question of being in love we have always been struck by the phenomenon of sexual overestimation - the fact that the loved object enjoys a certain amount of freedom from criticism, and that all its characteristics are valued more highly than those of people who are not loved, or that its own were at a time when it itself was not loved."[50] On a metapsychological level, when we love, "the object is being treated in the same way as our own ego, so that when we are in love a considerable amount of narcissistic libido overflows onto the object. It is even obvious, in many forms of love choice, that the object serves as a substitute for some unattained ego ideal of our own. We love it on account of the perfections which we have striven to reach for our own ego, and which we should now like to procure in this roundabout way as a means for satisfying our narcissism".[51] In sum, love arises from the cycle of identification and internalization which is the foundation for the sublimation that forges the social bond. When we are in love, "the object has taken the place of the ego ideal".[52] Freud is leading us to his famous formula: "A primary group... is a number of individuals who have substituted one and the same object for their ego ideal and have consequently identified themselves with one another in their ego".[53] But there is more to be said about this which points to a question Freud raises himself.

Because the question is crucial, it is worth quoting Freud in full:

> It is now easy to define the distinction between identification and such extreme developments of being in love as may be described as fascination or infatuation. In the former case the ego has enriched itself with the properties of the object, it has 'introjected' the object into itself, as Ferenczi expresses it. In the second case it is impoverished, it has surrendered itself to the object, it has substituted the object for its most important constituent. Closer consideration soon makes it plain, however, that this kind of account creates an illusion of contradistinctions that have no real existence. Economically there is no question of impoverishment or enrichment; it is even possible to describe an extreme case of being in love as a state in which the ego has introjected the object into itself. Another distinction is perhaps calculated to meet the essence of the matter. In the case of identification the object has been lost or given up; it is then set up again inside the ego, and the ego makes a partial alteration in itself after the model of the lost object. In the other case the object is retained, and there is a hyper-cathexis of it by the ego and at the ego's expense. But here again a difficulty presents itself. Is it quite certain that identification presupposes that object-cathexis has been given up? Can there be no identification with the object retained? And before we embark upon a discussion of this delicate question, the perception may already be beginning to dawn on us that yet another alternative embraces the real essence of the matter, namely, *whether the object is put in the place of the ego or of the ego ideal.* [54]

The "delicate" question Freud raises before he concludes this passage is at the heart of Freud's warning about love. Yet he shunts it aside and does not return to it in the text proper. Instead Freud pursues what he has termed "the real essence of the matter", taking us in a different direction that blunts the warning. He focuses our attention, in continuity with the italicized ending of the passage quoted above, on the case of the introjected object that is substituted for the abandoned one which holds the key to the social bond in primary groups. Primary groups, however, are different kinds of groups than Le Bon's groups which were the starting point for Freud's investigations. The question Freud raises but shunts aside implies the startling possibility that there can be "identification with the object retained" which we find stated nowhere else in his work. He insisted, rather, everywhere in his work that the history of each individual which leads through the Oedipus complex to a bond with the social group tracks the path of the original primal horde which has "left indestructible traces upon the history of human descent".[55] This always assumes an object cathexis given up with the object "set up again inside the ego..." The Law is preserved in the form of ego's struggle with the superego which forms the social bond that is modeled by the scene of the transference. Freud's question implies the possibility of a social bond formed out of an interdiction of the cycle at the the point at which the object cathexis should be abandoned and the object internalized - i.e., at the point of superego formation. Such a possibility goes far in explaining Le Bon's group. It also forces us to reconsider where exactly we are to locate the kind of group Le Bon describes in Freud's story about the origins of the social bond. The idea that Le Bon's groups, made up of individuals melded into something like a single body, are regressive phenomena suggests that we see in them traces of the beginning of the social bond. Yet the primal horde story, from which culture begins, does not begin with such a group as *its* beginning. Culture could not arise from the sequence of rebellion, murder and reparation, if the actions of the brothers, who initiate the sequence against the tyrannical father, represented the kind of unconstrained expression of the instincts which both Le Bon and Freud warn us characterizes the group behaving like an undifferentiated organism. The conflict between Eros and the death instinct, which the brothers' actions represent, places each instinct under constraints at the beginning. The primal horde story which Freud never stops insisting is the story of the beginning of culture, is the story of how these constraints play themselves out to result in the founding of culture. Put another way, in the beginning ambivalence between love and hate is already on the scene waiting to play itself out in the sequence of rebellion, murder, and reparation, whereas the kind of group Le Bon is concerned with is a group which "knows neither doubt nor uncertainty".[56] If we think of the primal horde story as the psychoanalytic version of the classic political idea of a social contract, then we can see that Le Bon's undifferentiated group cannot be located at the beginning of Freud's story of the social bond. Le Bon's group is a group because it already describes a social contract; but it is a social contract different from the one which governs the society which both Le Bon and Freud see it as menacing. Freud, in shifting the understanding of Le Bon's group to a psychoanalytic ground, has established a paradox which he is not to allude to until the end of the book, or more accurately, not until after the end of the book: Le Bon's group is, indeed, the sign of regression, but paradoxically, it is a regression which produces something new - a new kind of social contract. It is a group which belongs at the end of the story of the primal horde, which is to say, it points to the warning about love that supplies narrative closure to Freud's work. Le Bon was right to warn us about groups in which individuals are like hypnotized subjects, but he is right for reasons unknown to him which psychoanalysis illuminates. Le Bon's group does not depict the movement of history through which Eros pursues its ends, but a movement toward the end of history that signifies that the death instinct, using Eros, is asserting dominion over it.

Freud does not actually end "Group Psychology and the Analysis of the Ego" with this warning about love. Instead, he ends it by once more assuming the role of Freud the clinician. From this role he describes the drama played out between ego and superego on the "metapsychological" stage that tropes the mind leaving the connection unspoken between that drama and the one played out on the stage of the world as history. Despite the momentum of the book toward making that connection, he ends it as if everything he had said on the theory of groups had been meant to bear on the dynamics of a clinical disorder. The disorder this time is the one which exhibits "spontaneous oscillations of mood" that constitute "the displacement of a melancholia by a mania".[57] While there is much that is unknown about the mechanisms of this displacement, "on the basis of the analysis of the ego it cannot be doubted that in cases of mania the ego and the ego ideal have fused together, so that the person, in a mood of triumph and self satisfaction, disturbed by no self criticism, can enjoy the abolition of his inhibitions, his feelings of consideration for others, and his self reproaches".[58] The ego has disarmed the superego by using the heat of love to weld together all the actors on stage - ego, ego ideal and superego, into a single undifferentiated actor. This actor cannot make history. It is already at the end of history; a celebration of the end of desire. The fusion between the ego and the ego ideal in mania mimics the fusion of individuals in

Le Bon's group made up of individuals fused together through the dissolving of their boundaries. Le Bon's nightmare fuses with Freud's. There is only one act left - to end movement itself by laying waste to the world that is the stage on which things move. It is the Wolf Man as child obsessed with torturing everything that moves; obsessed with stopping the movement of the world that is the clock which keeps time. This is what Freud points to as he carries "Group Psychology and the Analysis of the Ego" beyond the somewhat disjointed discussion of whether the change into mania is or is not "an indispensable feature of the symptomatology of melancholic depression"[59] which poses as its last word.

It is a matter of following up "the delicate question" shunted aside in the main text, in the first of three postscripts presented like endnotes. Freud uses the army to illustrate the primary group whose bond he previously diagrammed as arising from an "identification of the ego with an object and replacement of the ego ideal with an object".[60] In other words, as arising from a love of the father which, when withdrawn from the father in a movement toward the narcissistic pole, carries the father with it, dooming that assertion of individuality to an endless struggle with the superego that includes returning the father to the world as a sublimated figure in relation to which the struggle goes on with the cycle ready to begin again. In the case of the army, "it is obvious that a soldier takes his superior, that is, really, the leader of the army, as his ideal... but he becomes ridiculous if he tries to identify himself with the general".[61] The soldier, in effect, knows who he is, in the sense of not having fused his ego with his ego ideal. The Catholic Church however, is used by Freud to return us to the possibility of Le Bon's groups which, by representing a fusion between ego and the idealized object it loves, carries a warning about love. "Every Christian loves Christ as his ideal and feels himself united with all other Christians by the tie of identification. But the Church requires more of him. He has also to identify himself with Christ and love all other Christians as Christ loved them. At both points, therefore, the Church requires that the position of the libido which is given by a group formation should be supplemented. Identification has to be added where object-choice has taken place, and object love where there is identification. This addition evidently goes beyond the constitution of the group".[62] Beyond to where and to what? Clearly to Le Bon's group. But this is, after all, only a postscript, and Freud has nothing further to say on the matter of identification added to object choice except to mute the warning by observing that most Christians are good Christians without adhering to "this further development in the distribution of libido in the group...".[63]

Freud, nevertheless, has prepared us to hear a warning about love with his analysis of Le Bon's group - the group mesmerized by the force of love, comprised of individuals that seem to have no will of their own, as if there were no boundaries between themselves and the leader, a group beyond that made up of soldiers who obey but know the difference between their desires and the desires of their general, a group confused over the otherwise distinct experiences of loving and being loved. The new "distribution of libido in the group" is a new social bond formed by extruding the father into the world *without internalizing him again*. Love is added to identification when ego submits itself to the extruded father in an act of love that dissolves its boundaries with him, in the model of the hypnotized to the hypnotizer.

We have returned to the theme of "The Ego and the Id": ego's need to be loved if it is to live. "Group Psychology and the Analysis of the Ego" adds to this theme that for ego to be loved means disarming its own ambivalence which can only lead to internalizing the father in another act of will which renews the struggle with the superego. Ego displays its disarmed ambivalence by displaying submission instead of struggle, by displaying the purity of its love as a piece, not a part, of a group, which Le Bon anxiously characterized as knowing "neither doubt nor uncertainty".[64] The final irony in ego's struggle with the superego is its bid to live by being loved: Ego submits to being the reflected image in the authorial mirror it once resisted being in an act of rebellious doubt. It is the death instinct that is released in Le Bon's regressive group. The new social bond is the sign of the death instinct assuming dominion over Eros by using Eros to reach the end of history which is made in the tension that fills the space between ego's boundary and the object of its ambivalent relationship. There is only one act left for which the group formed by this new social bond seems perfectly designed to accomplish: to lay waste the stage of the world on which history struggles to keep moving in its repetitive cycle that goes nowhere.

*

Freud's warning about love, arising from the transference moved into the world as the world, addresses no less than the question of what we must do to save the world. Why should we be surprised? Every psychoanalyst feels something like this solemn obligation when he undertakes to save his patient foundering in his own world. Freud's answer can only be in terms of the one work he ever calls on us to do, the work that is precisely identical to the work that gave rise to the warning about love which prompted it: to interpret the meaning of the world. It is this precise identity which gives his work its incomplete fragmented appearance. It is a work which does not give rise to a prophetic answer - i.e., to an answer that hangs the end of the world on a failure to fulfill a vision of possibility. Precisely the opposite. For Freud, interpreting the world means starting from where all interpretations start: confused meaning. But Freud's interpretations do not clarify meaning. While they fill in the conscious experience of a confused present with the past, they trace the scene of confused meaning that is the present to an original scene of confused meaning. Interpretation stops there because meaning itself arises as an effect of the instinctual drama taking place in the dark. Uncovering hidden meaning through interpretation does not cure confusion, pointing to possibilities confusion obscures. It uncovers an original confusion that repeats itself.

Few have stated this as succinctly and vividly as Philip Rieff: "For Freud, a given life history, even as a given group history, must be examined in terms of the experience of crucial events occurring necessarily at a specific historical time. What is crucial needs have happened early. There had to be a *Kairos*, that crucial time in the past that is decisive for what then must come after... For Freud, memory time is always kairotic... However, the Freudian understanding of Kairos is antithetical to the dynamic theological understanding. For Tillich, for example, Kairos is the break into a radically different future, into the fullness of time, providing new opportunity. But, for Freud, Kairos is, at most, the renaming of the past. The kairotic event has already happened; while in the radical theological understanding, Kairos is past only insofar as it has been manifest as a hint - even a proclamation - of the future."[65] We must however, if we are to be true to Freud, take it one further step which Rieff never takes. We need to represent the repetition of kairotic time as the sign of two instincts struggling in the dark to a standoff - repetition is confused movement whose purpose is to restrain purpose. It is this struggle in the dark, because it is struggle, which illuminates the confusion of the repetitive movement of passion as a tension which seeks to settle things, to release love from the grip of ambivalence, to have it exist like "war in classical periods... the moment it has been 'declared'".[66] Passion dreams of fleeing confusion, "no longer to unmask, no longer to interpret, but to make consciousness itself a drug, and thereby to accede to the perfect vision of reality, to the great bright dream, to prophetic love".[67] Freud sees in this, in his figurative language of the metapsychology, the ironic readiness of the ego to flee from the cruelty of the superego acceding to the demands of the death instinct which commands the superego's cruelty. Passion is always the self experiencing the painful confusion of being desire separated by obstacles it cannot control from what it knows will cure it of its pain. The need to straighten out its confusion is the sign of the death instinct's struggle for dominion over Eros, using love for this end. The work of consciousness defined by Freud's warning about love is a work that valorizes confusion, the sign that the struggle goes on, a standoff, confused movement without an end in sight.

At the end of his work, Freud turns its beginning on its head. No wonder he told H.D. several years after he published "Civilization and Its Discontents", "My discoveries are a basis for a very grave philosophy. There are very few who understand this, there are very few who are capable of understanding this."[68] And no wonder his socio-cultural texts are the least thought of, the most bowdlerized, the most ignored of his work. But because Freud treats Le Bon's groups, characterized by knowing neither doubt nor uncertainty, as a regression that produces a new social bond forged out of love, we cannot take his valorizing confusion lightly. Freud's warning about love carries the agenda of the twentieth century - an agenda brought into focus by the question Hannah Arendt posed: How shall we understand the banality of evil which wears the face of Adolf Eichmann?

Arendt's bold move was to give Eichmann's face to the question; to let the question emerge from the horror of the Final Solution. There were undoubtedly a lot of conscious and unconscious reasons for Arendt covering Eichmann's trial for the New Yorker. Elisabeth Young-Bruehl, in her indispensable if not definitive biography of Arendt, quotes her as calling it her *cura posterior*.[69] The critical focus of her analysis, however, carried by the subtitle of her book on the trial, "A Report on the Banality of Evil",[70] was to think against a number of thought systems whose narratives could not grasp the horror of the Final Solution. The prime target of Arendt, whose "first reaction to the 'man in the glass booth' in Jerusalem was that he was *nicht einmal unheimlich*, 'not even sinister', not inhuman or beyond comprehension"[71] was, of course, the Israeli prosecutor, Gideon Hausner's insistence Eichmann represented "the monster responsible"[72] for the horror piled upon horror that was the Final Solution. Arendt was not interested in arguing for anything less than Eichmann's responsibility, but rather, that thinking about that responsibilty could not be contained in what one reviewer of the prosecutor Hausner's own book on the trial called his "Manichean" vision of the Final Solution.[73] Neither was Arendt arguing against the unique horror of the Final Solution conveyed by its very name, in the sense that it might be considered an event for which other horrifics could be substituted. The term "banality of evil" is not meant to deny the singularity of the Final Solution as an ultimate horror, but to constitute it as a representation of an infinite number of possibilities that could fall under that title, by marking its source in an evil imminent in the social body which the social body itself regards as innocent of evil. It is meant to open a discourse on evil that shatters the narratives we have traditionally relied on to make the world coherent.

Arendt approached Eichmann on trial in Jerusalem with her own narrative developed in her major work, "The Origins of Totalitarianism". The thrust of that work, which Young-Bruehl accents in her inimitable summary of it, is socio-political. What pointed to the Nazi regime was the way

> "traditional social classes lost their specific class interests" and "those who became declasse inevitably came into contact with the superfluous residue of all classes: the mob, those Karl Marx had called the *Lumpenproletariat*, who had already fallen by the wayside in the bourgeoisie's triumph. When the declasse intellectual elites of the aristocracy and of the bourgeoisie encountered the mob, the elites and the mob discovered what they had in common: ferocious resentment of bourgeois hypocrisy and pretentiousness... Arendt's story of the deterioration of the state is woven together with her story of the loss, across all classes, of common interests and a shared world... The final turn from imperialism to totalitarianism came when the 'masses' following leaders cast up from the mob [like Hitler] or from their own ranks [like Himmler] become superfluous in an entirely unprecedented way. Individuals first become isolated within their classes, and then, as the classes themselves deteriorated from within, they become atomized and dehumanized. In the totalitarian machines of domination and extermination , 'the masses of coordinated philistines' provided the most efficient and ignominious functionaries."[74]

But Arendt was unable to maintain her narrative as staunchly socio-political. It foundered on the boundaries it could not sustain between the sociological and the psychological, which Freud insisted from the other direction in "Group Psychology and the Analysis of the Ego" are illusory. "When she wrote 'What is Existenz Philosophy?' Arendt had called the result of the story 'egoism'; when she wrote as a historian she called it 'bourgeois individualism'; later as a political theorist, she used the term 'world alienation'".[75] Yet Arendt never shows an interest in psychology, more or less the depth psychology of psychoanalysis. The "banality of evil" comes down to a gloss on "the philistine" as she put it, who is "the bourgeois isolated from his own class, the atomized individual who is produced by the breakdown of the bourgeois class itself... [He is] the bourgeois who in the midst of the ruins of his world worried about nothing so much as his private security, [and] was ready to sacrifice everything - belief, honor, dignity - on the slightest provocation."[76]

The banality of evil is reduced in her narrative to a "revolt of the masses against common sense...";[77] the banality of stupid beliefs. She does not recognize the ironies Freud associates with the ego's desperate try to live by being loved - self-respect through sacrifice. While she stresses "that attempts to view totalitarianism within traditional frameworks would lead to misunderstanding"[78] she avoids calling it passion's struggle to realize an ominous vision of possibility. Yet what is it she describes but that? Totalitarianism invents nothing new. The particulars of its political structures and its lame ideologies are fueled by a single vision of possibility that has always been able to command love: life begins with me. Totalitarianism envisions, in Arendt's terms, that "the law of Nature or the law of History, if properly executed, is expected to produce mankind as its end product".[79] Everything that has been has been confusion shamming as life, the lack of what is vivifying. Life cannot begin until a love is declared which dissolves boundaries, cancels distinctions, fuses things together which are usually thought of as different. Totalitarianism "substitutes for the boundaries and channels of communication between individual men a band of iron which hold them so tightly together that it is as though their plurality had disappeared into One Man of gigantic dimensions".[80]

She approaches Eichmann as banal stupidity, not passion. He is "an inability to *think*, namely to think from the standpoint of somebody else",[81] but never considers that the truth of the matter may be just the opposite - viz., that he may be unable to think except from the standpoint of somebody else. She sees him as a clown, the sadly comic figure in which "the horrible can be not only ludicrous but outright funny";[82] a confused subject "with complete lack of consistency in his thoughts and sentiments"[83]; someone who appeared to have a "taped memory that showed itself to be proof against reason and argument and information and insight of any kind".[84] What Arendt did not see was that de Rougemont, for example, would have no trouble seeing in this series a figure of passion. It would have to be a figure of passion in the chilling modern sense recognized by Freud as the obsessive character structure - passion in the form of the cool calculations of the deliria of rationality, something like the calculations displayed by the Rat Man over paying back the captain for his package, but without the Rat Man's tormented obsessive doubts and uncertainties.

Eichmann represents a passion with a certainty of love that has forged a new social bond. He is not the passion fueled by an agony of ambivalence, but the ego already fleeing its boundaries to disarm the cruelty of the superego by becoming its abject slave, like the hypnotized to the hypnotist. Arendt focusing on the marginal, hears the strange proviso in Eichmann's plea of guilty which no one else apparently heard: "Not guilty in the sense of the indictment", and asks "In what sense... did he think he was guilty?"[85] Put another way, what did Eichmann think was on trial? He did not seem to think, as did the Israelis, that his acts which measured his evil intentions, desires, will were on trial. He was at least honest about this: "He did not want to be one of those who now pretended that 'they had always been against it,' whereas in fact they had been very eager to do what they were told to do... What he had done he had done, he did not want to deny it; rather he proposed 'to hang myself in public as warning example for all anti-Semites on this earth.' By this he did not mean to say that he regretted anything: 'Repentance is for little children.'"[86] Arendt notes that throughout the trial, Eichmann tried to clarify what he meant by his strange plea, "mostly without success". What she heard, was that for Eichmann "the indictment implied not only that he acted on purpose , which he did not deny, but out of base motives and in full knowledge of the criminal nature of his deeds. As for the base motives, he was perfectly sure that he was not what he called an *innerer Schweinehund*, a dirty bastard in the depths of his heart; and as for his conscience, he remembered perfectly well that he would have had a bad conscience only if he had not done what he had been ordered to do..." [87]

For Eichmann, at the center of his trial was the purity of his heart measured by his devotion and love. He could not have had a bad conscience, because he did not have a conscience in the sense of an internalized imago of the father toward which ego has ambivalent relations. His conscience had been extruded into the world where it was indistinguishable from his ego. Arendt, with her shrewd ability to read between the lines seems to have sensed precisely this when she heard Eichmann testify "that he had lived his whole life according to Kant's moral precepts...".[88] This was not, for Arendt the testimony of an outrageous liar. She heard instead, that Eichmann had acted in accord with "Hans Frank's formulation of the 'categorical imperative' in the Third Reich...: Act in such a way that the Fuhrer, if he knew your action, would approve it".[89] Eichmann's claim that he was "an 'idealist'... not merely a man who believed in an 'idea'..." but "a man who lived for his idea - hence he could not be a businessman - and who was prepared to sacrifice for his idea everything and, especially, everybody",[90] was more than a statement by the banal figure of a clown who had no ability to make sensible judgments. Was it even his idea he had made sacrifices for? Indeed, had he ever had an idea that could be called his from the day he joined the S.S.? Eichmann had entered that dark region of love which lies beyond the bonds of the soldier to his leader. He had gone beyond "the mere call of obedience [to] identify his own will with the principle behind the law - the source from which the law sprang".[91]

It is true that by the end of Arendt's book, Eichmann the man remains a puzzle, just as Germany itself does, and indeed, as Arendt herself pointed out, bringing down a storm of abuse, just as the Jewish victims remain a puzzle. Who, in the latter half of the twentieth century, cannot hear himself echoing Bauman's confession that "what did happen was far too complicated to be explained in that simple and intellectually comforting way I naively imagined sufficient. I realized that the Holocaust was not only sinister and horrifying, but also an event not at all easy to comprehend in habitual, 'ordinary' terms. This event had been written down in its own code which had to be broken first to make understanding possible".[92] In a sense, the Final Solution is the ultimate patient of our time, a subject waiting its Freud to grasp the excess of that horror which overflows our attempts to make sense of it.

Freud's warning about love is a starting point, opening the door to understanding love as the banality of evil imminent in the very fibers of the social bond which has throughout history intertwined the sublime with violence. Love fuels the visions of kitsch that the social body always seems ready to chase when it is most afraid. "In ordinary kitsch" Friedlander points out, "there is an equivalence between the representation of reality and what could exist in reality: lovers actually do lie under a fir tree like two turtle doves; a cottage from whose chimney a thin tendril of smoke rises could indeed harbor a happy family; a Swiss landscape does resemble a picture postcard." Yet ordinary kitsch leaves doubt at the heart of the harmony it represents, precisely because it insists on referring us back to the "reality" of this world. Ordinary kitsch is love plagued with doubt. In dealing with transference love, every analyst knows that he can expect assistance from the patient's resistance to the kitschy images with which the patient tries to flood their relationship. But not every kitsch is "ordinary". "Faced with a kitsch representation of death, everyone knows that here two contradictory elements are amalgamated: on the one hand, an appeal to harmony, to emotional communion at the simplest and most immediate level; on the other, solitude and terror... Basically, at the level of individual experience, kitsch and death remain incompatible."[93] It is when these amalgamated images no longer refer us to "what is" as the real, but refer us instead to "what is" as a preface to a real that is yet to be that "the juxtaposition of these two contradictory elements represents the foundation of a certain religious aesthetic...".[94] It is the Nazi aesthetic which Friedlander is speaking of, not in the sense of a historical aberration that has been left behind, but in the sense in which Arendt finds the Eichmann we keep insisting is indescribable to be banal.

Freud's warning about love as a sign of the death instinct's assuming dominion over Eros defines a work of consciousness that valorizes confusion by putting the love we cannot stop repeating under the sign of suspicion. It is only when we see the confusion of our passions as the structure of life itself, not as our life waiting to be straightened out by the discovery of love - the universal medicine against which Freud warns us, that we can feel we are preserving life. Freud would no doubt not deny Kristeva the validity, as far as it goes, of asserting that "it is want of love that sends the subject into analysis", or that "the analytic situation is the only place explicitly provided in the social contract in which we are allowed to talk about the wounds we have suffered and to search for possible new identities and new ways of talking about ourselves".[95] Neither would he probably deny her asserting that the therapeutic discourse makes a difference if at the end "fantasy returns to our psychic life, but no longer as cause for complaint or source of dogma. Now it provides the energy for a kind of artifice, for the art of living".[96] But Freud would insist that if living is an art, all we create out of the art of life is a pentimento. We can neither stop generating visions of the possibilities of our life, or of loving the visions we generate; but the work of consciousness is to cast everything we love under the sign of suspicion. The art of life must be the cultivation of confusion, ambivalence and doubt in order to keep life alive.

We cannot underestimate the power of doubt, the confusion that intercepts its own visions of straightening itself out. Neither Freud nor Sartre, both of whom in different ways hated solitude but never stopped being figures of solitude, could avoid keeping doubt alive while dreaming love's ambitious dreams. Freud was always the compulsive lover. Adler was his Fliess, although he would never admit that he sought to fall in love with Adler as he sought to fall in love with Fliess who wanted to supply the last word for a psychoanalysis not yet fully born. Freud's love for both was a disaster, because Freud's revisionists always carried the burden of what he did not want to hear from them: the burden of his own last word. As for Sartre, he could never escape being haunted by the absurd with which he started, although at the end it was not the source of nausea that it was at the beginning. At the age of seventy, having difficulty walking, with high blood pressure and nearly blind, he is asked by an interviewer: "So far life has been good to you?" He replies: "On the whole, yes. I don't see what I could reproach it with. It has given me what I wanted and at the same time it has shown that it wasn't much. But what can you do?" The transcript reports that at this point "the interview ends in wild laughter brought on by the last statement." Sartre concludes: "The laughter must be kept. You should put: 'Accompanied by laughter'".[97] It should not go unnoticed that Freud taught us that laughter is the serious sound that follows a last word, throwing doubt on it.

At the same time, we cannot overestimate the power of doubt. With a work of consciousness that doubts everything that is loved, we must learn to love doubt. We must learn to live the confusion of fearing the dark and fearing being without it. Children know that ambivalence intimately. Did not Sartre point that out with Emily? And what else are we until something happens, and who knows what or when?

References

1 J. Laplanche and J-B Pontalis, *The Language of Psychoanalysis*, tr. by Donald Nicholson-Smith, New York, W.W.Norton, 1973, p. 50.

2 Sigmund Freud, "The Ego and the Id", *Standard Edition*, V. 19, p. 18.

3 Ibid., p. 24.

4 Ibid., p. 25.

5 Ibid., p. 59.

6 Ibid., p. 46.

7 Ibid., p. 30.

8 Ibid., p. 40.

9 Ibid., p. 46.

10 Ibid., p. 47.

11 Ibid., p. 34.

12 Ibid., p. 34.

13 Ibid., p. 56.

14 Ibid., p. 56.

15 Ibid., p. 58.

16 Ibid., p. 58.

17 Ibid., p. 59.

18 Ibid., p. 59.

19 Sigmund Freud, "Civilization and Its Discontents", *Standard Edition*, V. 21, p. 145.

20 Ibid., p. 64.

21 Ibid., p. 64.

22 Ibid., p. 64.

23 Ibid., p. 65-66.

24 Ibid., p. 66.

25 Ibid., p. 76.

26 Ibid., p. 76.

27 Robert A. Nisbet, *Social Change and History*, London, Oxford University Press, 1969, p. 3.

28 Sigmund Freud, SE, 21, p. 97.

29 Ibid., p. 101.

30 Ibid., p. 101.

31 Quoted in Raymond Boudon, *The Analysis of Ideology*, tr. Malcolm Slater, The University of Chicago Press, 1986, p. 17.

32 J. Hillis Miller, "Narrative", in Frank Lentricchia and Thomas McLaughlin (eds.), *Critical Terms for Literary Study*, Chicago, The University of Chicago Press, 1990, p. 72.

33 Sigmund Freud, SE, 21, p. 122.

34 Quoted in J. Laplanche and J.-B. Pontalis, *The Language of Psychoanalysis*, p. 73.

35 Sigmund Freud, SE, 21, p. 127.

36 Ibid., p. 125.

37 Ibid., p. 127-128.

38 Ibid., p. 129.

39 Ibid., p. 129.

40 Ibid., p. 129.

41 Ibid., p. 129-130.

42 Ibid., p. 132.

43 Quoted in Kenneth Burke, *On Symbols and Society*, ed. Joseph R. Gusfield, Chicago, The University of Chicago Press, 1989, p. 257.

44 Sigmund Freud, "Group Psychology and the Analysis of the Ego", *Standard Edition*, V. 18, p. 129.

45 Ibid., p. 72.

46 Ibid., p. 74.

47 Ibid., p. 75-76.

48 Ibid., p. 92.

49 Ibid., p. 105.

50 Ibid., p. 112.

51 Ibid., p. 112.

52 Ibid., p. 113.

53 Ibid., p. 116.

54 Ibid., p. 113-114.

55 Ibid., p. 122.

56 Ibid., p. 78.

57 Ibid., p. 132.

58 Ibid., p. 132.

59 Ibid., p. 132.

60 Ibid., p. 134.

61 Ibid., p. 134.

62 Ibid., p. 134.

63 Ibid., p. 135.

64 Ibid., p. 78.

65 Philip Rieff, "The Meaning of History and Religion in Freud's Thought", in Bruce Mazlish (ed.), *Psychoanalysis and History*, Revised Edition, New York, Grosset and Dunlap, 1971, p. 26-27.

66 Denis de Rougemont, *Love Declared: Essays on the Myths of Love*, tr. Richard Howard, New York, Pantheon Books, p. 19.

67 Roland Barthes, *A Lover's Discourse: Fragments*, tr. Richard Howard, New York, Hill and Wang, 1978, p. 60.

68 Quoted in Stanley Edgar Hyman, *The Tangled Bank*, New York, Atheneum, 1962, p. 407.

69 Elisabeth Young-Bruehl, *Hannah Arendt: For Love of the World*, New Haven, Yale University Press, 1982, p. 329.

70 Hannah Arendt, *Eichmann in Jerusalem: A Report on the Banality of Evil*, New York, The Viking Press, 1963.

71 Elisabeth Young-Bruehl, *Hannah Arendt: For Love of the World*, p. 329.

72 Hannah Arendt, *Eichmann in Jerusalem*, p. 6.

73 Elisabeth Young-Bruehl, *Hannah Arendt: For Love of the World*, p. 358.

74 Ibid., p. 219-221.

75 Ibid., p. 220.

76 Ibid., p. 221.

77 Ibid., p. 221.

78 Ibid., p. 290.

79 Hannah Arendt, *Eichmann in Jerusalem*, p. 160.

80 Ibid., p. 163-164.

81 Ibid., p. 44.

82 Ibid., p. 43.

83 Ibid., p. 57.

84 Ibid., p. 72.

85 Ibid., p. 19.

86 Ibid., p. 21.

87 Ibid., p. 22.

88 Ibid., p. 120.

89 Ibid., p. 121.

90 Ibid., p. 37.

91 Ibid., p. 121.

92 Zygmunt Bauman, *Modernity and the Holocaust*, Ithaca, New York, Cornell University Press, 1989, p. vi-vii.

93 Saul Friedlander, *Reflections on Nazism*, tr. Thomas Weyr, New York, Harper and Row, 1984, p. 26-27.

94 Ibid., p. 27.

95 Julia Kristeva, *In the Beginning was Love: Psychoanalysis and Faith*, tr. Arthur Goldhammer, New York, Columbia University Press, 1987, p. 3.

96 Ibid., p. 9.

97 Jean-Paul Sartre, *Life/Situations: Essays Written and Spoken*, tr. Paul Auster and Lydia Davis, New York, Pantheon Books, 1977, p. 92.

Permission Credits

Reprinted from *Group Psychology and the Analysis of the Ego* by Sigmund Freud, Translated and Edited by James Strachey, by permission of W.W. Norton & Company, Inc. Copyright 1959 by Sigmund Freud Copyrights Ltd. Copyright 1959 by James Strachey. Translation and editorial matter copyright 1959, 1922 by the Institute of Psycho-Analysis and Angela Richards. Copyright renewed 1987.

Reprinted from *Beyond the Pleasure Principle* by Sigmund Freud, Translated and Edited by James Strachey, by permission of W.W. Norton & Company, Inc. Copyright 1961 by James Strachey. Copyright renewed 1989.

Reprinted from *Civilization and its Discontents* by Sigmund Freud, Translated and Edited by James Strachey, by permission of W.W. Norton & Company, Inc. Copyright 1961 by James Strachey. Copyright renewed 1989.

Reprinted from *The Ego and The Id* by Sigmund Freud, Translated by Joan Riviere, Revised and Edited by James Strachey, by permission of W.W. Norton & Company, Inc. Copyright 1960 by James Strachey. Copyright renewed 1989 by Alix Strachey.

Reprinted from *Group Psychology and the Analysis of the Ego,* by permission of Sigmund Freud Copyrights, The Institute of Psycho-Analysis and The Hogarth Press for permission to quote from *The Standard Edition of the Complete Psychological Works of Sigmund Freud*, translated and edited by James Strachey.

Reprinted from *Notes Upon a Case of Obsessional Neurosis*, by permission of Sigmund Freud Copyrights, The Institute of Psycho-Analysis and The Hogarth Press for permission to quote from *The Standard Edition of the Complete Psychological Works of Sigmund Freud*, translated and edited by James Strachey.

Reprinted from *Civilization and its Discontents*, by permission of Sigmund Freud Copyrights, The Institute of Psycho-Analysis and The Hogarth Press for permission to quote from *The Standard Edition of the Complete Psychological Works of Sigmund Freud*, translated and edited by James Strachey.

Reprinted from *The Ego and The Id*, by permission of Sigmund Freud Copyrights, The Institute of Psycho-Analysis and The Hogarth Press for permission to quote from *The Standard Edition of the Complete Psychological Works of Sigmund Freud*, translated and edited by James Strachey.

Reprinted from *From the History of an Infantile Neurosis* by permission of Sigmund Freud Copyrights, The Institute of Psycho-Analysis and The Hogarth Press for permission to quote from *The Standard Edition of the Complete Psychological Works of Sigmund Freud*, translated and edited by James Strachey.

Reprinted from *Beyond the Pleasure Principle* by permission of Sigmund Freud Copyrights, The Institute of Psycho-Analysis and The Hogarth Press for permission to quote from *The Standard Edition of the Complete Psychological Works of Sigmund Freud*, translated and edited by James Strachey.

Reprinted from *The Ego and The Mechanisms of Defense*, by Anna Freud, translated by Cecil Baines, New York, International Universities Press, Inc, 1946, by permission of International Universities Press, Inc.

Reprinted from *Critique of Dialectical Reason* by Jean-Paul Sartre, by permission of VERSO, 6 Meard Street, London WIV 3HR, United Kingdom.

Reprinted from *The Family Idiot:Gustave Flaubert*, V.1 & V.2 by Jean-Paul Sartre, Translated by Darol Cosman, by permission of the University of Chicago Press, 1981.

Reprinted from *Baudelaire* by Jean-Paul Sartre, translated by Martin Turnell, Copyright 1950, New Directions Publishing, Corp. Reprinted by permission of New Directions Publishing, Corp.

Excerpts from *Being and Nothingness* by Jean-Paul Sartre, Translated by Hazel E. Barnes, reprinted by permission of Allied Books, Ltd, 31 W. 21st Street, New York, NY 10010.

Excerpts from *Being-in-the-World, Selected Papers of Ludwig Binswanger*, edited and introduced by Jacob Needleman. Copyright 1963 by Basic Books Inc. Reprinted by permission of Basic Books, a division of HarperCollins Publishers.

Reprinted from *Hannah Arendt: For Love of the World* by Elisabeth Young-Bruehl, New Haven, Yale University Press, 1982, by permission of Elisabeth Young-Breuhl.

Reprinted from *Eichmann in Jerusalem: A Report on the Banality of Evil,* by Hannah Arendt, New York, The Viking Press, 1963, by permission of Penguin USA.

Reprinted from *Freud and Philosophy* by Paul Ricoeur, translated by Denis Savage, New Haven, Yale University Press 1970 by permission of Yale University Press.

The Reshaping of Psychoanalysis
From Sigmund Freud to Ernest Becker

This series is designed to offer works which are concerned with the reshaping and revitalization of psychoanalysis. Also critical to this series is the interweaving of such disciplines as psychology, psychiatry, religion, and philosophy so as to promote dialogue and offer avenues toward rapprochement.

This series will publish and proffer studies of Freud and Neo-Freudians such as Becker which are most aware of the long term contributions of psychoanalysis toward the healing of self and society. Studies should be scholarly and clinically discerning. This is a series which is keenly concerned with the bridging of disciplines, the networking of ideas and peoples, and with the perpetuation of the psychoanalytic questions, and, at times, its answers. This is a series which is also very open to its authors' creativity and most appreciative of those efforts which reshape, revamp, revitalize, and transform Freudian psychoanalysis.

The General Series Editor is Barry R. Arnold. Dr. Arnold is an associate professor of Religious Studies and Philosophy at the University of West Florida. His speciality area is psychoanalysis and medical ethics.

DATE DUE			
			Printed in USA